INSPIRED
IDEAS FOR

_____

*The journey of creating
a home is your unique and
inspiring adventure!*

THE
Inspired
ROOM

MELISSA
MICHAELS

HARVEST HOUSE PUBLISHERS
EUGENE, OREGON

The Inspired Room

Text copyright © 2015 by Melissa Michaels
Photography copyright © 2015 by Melissa Michaels

Published by Harvest House Publishers
Eugene, Oregon 97402
www.harvesthousepublishers.com

ISBN 978-0-7369-6309-1 (hardcover)
ISBN 978-0-7369-6310-7 (eBook)

Cover and interior design by Faceout Studio, Bend, Oregon
Original illustrations by Nicole Johnson

Published in association with William K. Jensen Literary Agency, 119 Bampton Court, Eugene, Oregon 97404.

Printed in China

18 19 20 21 22 23 / DS – FO / 10 9 8 7 6 5 4 3

To the loyal followers of
The Inspired Room blog.

Thank you from
the bottom of my heart.

CREATE A HOME
inspired
BY YOUR life
& WHAT YOU love
AND THEN YOUR HOME WILL
inspire you

CONTENTS

My House

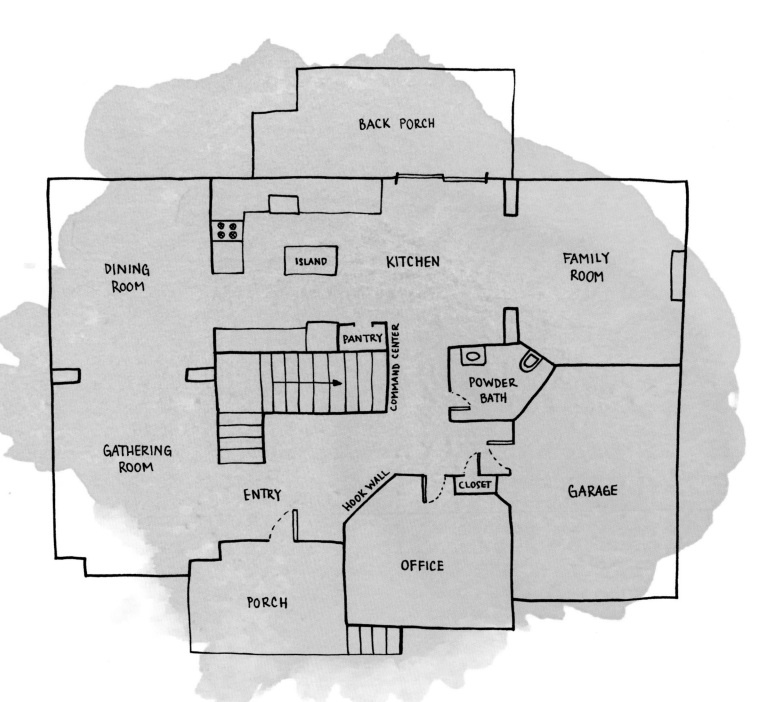

FIRST FLOOR

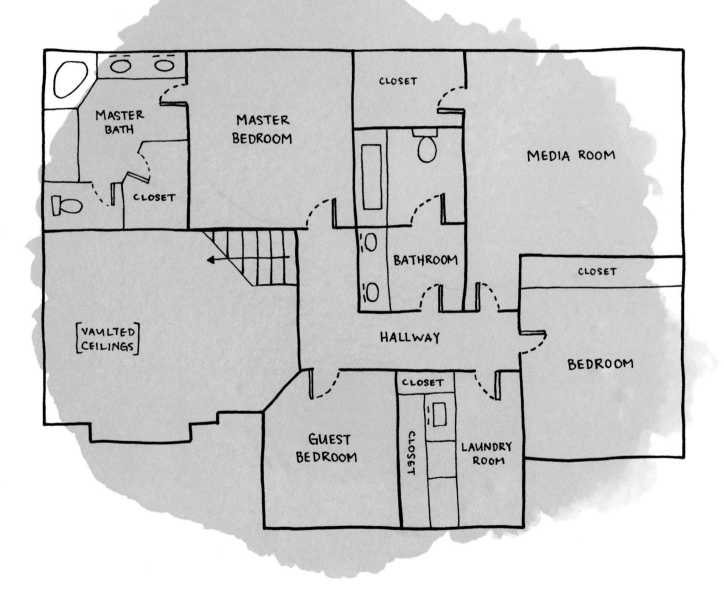

MASTER BATH

MASTER BEDROOM

CLOSET

MEDIA ROOM

CLOSET

BATHROOM

VAULTED CEILINGS

CLOSET

HALLWAY

BEDROOM

GUEST BEDROOM

CLOSET

CLOSET

LAUNDRY ROOM

SECOND FLOOR

Creating a Retreat

{Introduction}

Think of your ultimate getaway. You know, that special place you envision as an escape from the cares and stress of the world. Maybe it's a quaint cottage on the coast or a gorgeous mountain lodge where you can slow down, inhale fresh air, and be rejuvenated with an inspired perspective. While it's wonderful to head off on a vacation to recharge, what if you could create that same sense of a retreat every day right where you are?

I believe our home can be a daily destination for relaxation and reenergizing when it's filled with meaningful and intentional beauty. Our home should inspire us to go out into the world to do the great things we dream of and then welcome us back for refreshment, just like we'd want to experience at our favorite getaway.

What we see around us right now may make us question whether it's even possible to turn our home into the oasis we long for, but it is possible. If we start with a sense of purpose and intention for the home we want, we won't end up at a destination that doesn't make sense for our needs. We will end up with a retreat that reflects who we are and what matters most to us.

This book is for you if you ever find yourself dazed or confused, wondering how to move forward with the design of your home when there are so many possibilities, so little time and money…and so much potential for ending up with a random mix of impulsive, regrettable choices.

Getting There Is the Fun Part

START HERE

Make a list of the many things you like, and celebrate the joy of choices and decisions. Along this journey together, you'll discover more starting places to help you move toward a home that inspires you.

How do you get there, to that home you picture in your dreams? Is it even possible with the home you have? I've pondered those questions with my readers for more than eight years at The Inspired Room online.

While I dreamed of a beautiful home, I wasn't quite sure how to get there. As you probably do, I have hand-me-downs and objects and pieces I've collected over time. And because I like so many styles and design ideas, when I tried to evolve *my* style I felt as if my home was going in every direction. I was that crazy-eyed, indecisive woman who would flip through magazines, peruse Pinterest, head out to shop, and become overwhelmed by possibilities!

I like white. I like dark. I like color.

I like texture. I like peaceful. I like lively.

I like serious. I like fun.

I like clean and fresh surfaces. I like contrast.

I like a mix of styles and colors all in one room.

I like informal. I like cozy. I like modern. I like pretty.

I like quality and well-designed pieces.
(But, darn, I don't have the budget for high-end furniture.)

I like dignified. I like classy. But then again, I like quirky.
But I don't like tacky. And sometimes
there is a fine line between quirky-fun and tacky.

FOR THE LOVE. Why can't I make a decision?

Do you have design ADD too?

While patience has been and will be required, I get great joy from each small change and step along the way. The good news is that I no longer feel quite so *haphazard* about what I need or want to do with this house. I still love many styles, but the decisions are easier to make now, and I savor the process of refining and evolving my home in new ways.

Enjoy the journey. Just as you grow and change, your home should too.

Creating an Authentic Home

Shaping one home over time is an entirely different experience than having a professional design a house from top to bottom with a large budget and a completion date.

As a result of my own experience, this isn't a typical design book filled with professional images of beautiful projects from an interior designer's portfolio. You won't find design ideas that require admittance to a designer showroom. This isn't an interior design manual at all, but rather encouraging inspiration to create a real home you love and love to live in.

Creating an authentic home is the slow process of learning to pay attention to what speaks to you and how your home *feels* to you. It invites you to embrace (and appreciate) the joy found even in the smallest details and improvements along the way.

This isn't about following the rules or style trends that someone who has never been in your home tells you to adhere to. It is about rediscovering the simple ways you can tend to, brighten up, and personalize your home.

Your Home, Your Look

So how do you pull your own look together, especially if you are working with a home's imperfections and things you have gathered over time? I have a lot of experience with that, so I'll show you how! I'll share the simple tips and style discoveries I've used to create a home I love, one that is authentic to my family and reflects the way we live. To help orient you to our space, I included the upstairs and downstairs floor plans after the table of contents.

While this book will introduce you to my family's home, my goal is to encourage and spark ideas for your home. You may share my style or we may have completely different design preferences, but no matter what kind of home you dream of, I'm happy to share my lessons learned and offer practical ideas to create the home of *your* dreams.

There isn't any pressure here to keep up with the trends or decorate for show. By surrounding yourself with beautiful things you actually use and love, you will experience more joy in everyday activities. You'll spend less money decorating. And as a happy result, you shape an attractive home effortlessly, without trying hard to "decorate."

The journey of creating a home is your unique and inspiring adventure!

Everyday on Display

Years ago I started using a phrase to describe my simple approach to everyday decorating: *everyday on display* (not to be confused with *everyday in disarray*, heh). To me, this means less-fussy styling, simpler beauty, and a deeper appreciation of the things I use and see every day. We may as well love to use what we have in our home because it makes everyday tasks more enjoyable!

With this philosophy, even simple things we collect, such as books, movie tickets, postcards, and art from travels, and special quotes that mean something to us, can become a part of our style when we intentionally incorporate them into our decor. Our home has evolved over time with a mix of things we've been given, pieces we found at flea markets and secondhand stores, and memories we collected one story at a time. A home that evolves will have a unique character.

A Worthwhile Journey

I take pleasure in the journey of creating a home I love. You'll see through these pages how I mix and match what we have, how I bring color into my home, how I use lighting to set the mood, and how I gave each room a unique purpose and look.

You'll find images I took of my home so I could invite you into each and every room. Well, to be clear, I took photos of every room but one—my master bathroom. It remains on my to-do list, where it has been for quite some time! Our house has come a long way, but there is still more to do. It's a real home. That is one of the many confessions you'll read throughout this book in my "keeping it real" confessions.

I believe a home isn't a showplace—it's a sanctuary. And the journey of creating that space is worthy and wonderful. I hope that opening my home to you encourages you to look at your own in a fresh way and maybe even nudge you to try something new—or something you've been dreaming about—to create a home you'll love.

1

First Impressions

{ The Entryway }

An entryway is the space that extends a warm "welcome home" to your family at the end of a long day away and a sincere "we're glad you're here" to the people invited into your sanctuary. The entry provides a glimpse into the life we live within our own four walls. And if, at times, it reveals a bit too much about us, that's okay too. When we're authentic, we invite our guests to be themselves. That's hospitality at its best.

With two wildly exuberant but adorable doodle pups at our house, the chances of me opening the front door to greet a visitor without a commotion are slim. As I invite you in, let me set the scene. For several chaotic minutes, Jack and Lily will invariably fling themselves in the air and tug on your coat (I know, they failed obedience school). Then they will run up and down the stairs to show off their agility.

Once the pups are past the initial excitement of your arrival (by now I'm sweating and my hair is standing on end) and you're welcomed in, your first

DISCOVER THE IMPACT OF SIMPLE CHANGES

MAKE THE MOST OF YOUR ENTRY, NO MATTER THE SIZE

DIY—REPURPOSE A JUG INTO A LAMP

impression is likely that we live with a bit of imperfect chaos. Yes. Yes, we do. But we also live life with gusto (and with fur flying), so I hope you'll also notice the happy, casual, and lively home we have here—a home designed to welcome people and pups alike.

Whether you have a defined entryway or your front door opens directly into a living room, this is the welcoming space that starts to tell the story of you and your family. It begins with an authentic impression and an invitation to relax so the whole story can unfold in greater detail, room by room.

Choose Your Focal Point

When you first walk into your home, does a focal point capture your attention? Artwork, mirror, tall plant, or fun piece of furniture? There are great benefits to creating a focal point. Believe me, it's better to have a guest zoom in on one intentional, attractive feature than to become distracted by clutter (ahem) or elements that don't yet reflect your style.

- Focal points can be moveable pieces. Try a striking table, cabinet, or bench. If you don't have room for furniture, use a bold mirror to grab attention and reflect light around the room or collections of photos in frames for a personal touch. If your entry opens right into another room, make the focal point in the adjoining space as welcoming as possible.

- Go for bigger objects or wall hangings rather than several little items.

- Use at least one interesting piece that gets people talking! Look around your house and see what conversation piece you could put in your entry.

When we first moved in to this home, we were eager to put our own stamp of style on the generic builder-style house. There was a no-paint policy during the nine months while we rented, but this gave me time to decide that I wanted to paint our focal point. As soon as we bought the house, we happily painted wide horizontal stripes on our entry wall. This creative focal point made the entryway feel intentional and defined.

What currently catches your eye when you enter your home? If it isn't something you intended to steal the visual show, like a pile of shoes, then decide which piece, paint, plant, etc. could be added.

START HERE

Enter your home through your front door right now. Look at the entry with fresh eyes. What does it say to your family and guests as they come in?

+ Does it set the tone and atmosphere you want for your home?

+ What about your space doesn't work well?

+ What is there too much of, what is there too little of?

Find DIY instructions for painting horizontal stripes in chapter six, "A Functional Space."

Just the Right Piece

The right piece is worth waiting for. We may think it's best to have everything all at once, but that pressure can make us crazy and cause us to miss out on the beautiful unfolding of our home's look and story.

For quite a while, I didn't bring new additions into my house because I wanted to weed out what didn't suit us so I could wait and watch for pieces that did. When my daughter and I spotted an adorable dresser at a secondhand store, we knew it was *the* piece to set the tone for our entryway and home. It had the cottage vibe and a touch of class with metal hardware and a rounded front. Best of all, I didn't have to paint it because it was already cute. Score.

Connect Rooms with Color

In our entry, we established our style and started a flow of color. The white entry dresser ties in with other pieces in our home—our powder room vanity, our dining room table, a secretary and hutch in my office, and painted rattan chairs in the kitchen. The paint colors of our horizontal stripes, also found elsewhere in our home, set the stage for our home's color palette.

Unifying colors can be presented in easy-to-change extras, such as a bouquet of flowers, seasonal table runners, or a colorful stack of books. Repeating colors throughout your home creates a familiar flow and expands the confines of the entry to welcome people into your home.

Creating a home we love takes time and intention. Those items we patiently look for often end up having more significance and purpose.

KEEPING IT REAL

Our entry stripes were done incorrectly! The stripes at the top and bottom are not of equal size. Good news: We have perfectly sized stripes in our TV room now and those can be your best "after" example!

1 Add a lamp or candles to give your entry a warm glow at night. Dark entries are depressing and not functional. Find lighting with a great shape and personality to suit your style.

2 Layer objects such as books, baskets, old trunks, crates, or footstools under open tables and benches to give a cozier feel. Corral smaller items in a tray to bring more order.

3 Stack books or use footed plates or pedestals on tabletops to bring more warmth and height to accessories. Lean art or mirrors for a stylish look.

4 Make a creative coat hanger for your wall with just about anything (shutters, an old door, a wooden step ladder, or even a weathered plank of wood) and a few functional, attractive hooks.

5 Place the top of your wainscoting at least one-third of the way up the wall or about 36 inches from the floor. If you will add hooks, shoulder height is a reasonable measure.

6 Warm up the space with textured wallpaper or wood walls, or go super simple and add a cozy patterned or textured rug.

🐾 **TIP:** Indoor/outdoor rugs are easy to keep clean, even with dogs. When they get dirty, I wipe them off with a rag or take them outside and hose them down (the rugs, not the dogs).

Everyday on Display— Style and Storage to Go

Storage doesn't have to be in the form of an ugly plastic tote! It can be a fun yellow leather bag or polka-dotted canvas one! Bags hung on hooks can be ever-changing, colorful sources of storage for grab-and-go items. I scour Target sales for bags that suit my style and needs.

Think about your specific, regular needs. I have one bag designated for church every Sunday. During the week, I add to it what I'll need so I won't leave things behind. Routines make life so much easier and cute bags make life so much more enjoyable.

Embellish!

{OVERHEAD LIGHT FIXTURE}

No one would consider me a DIY diva. But I might accept the imaginary honor of being titled an embellishment diva. I have fun taking an item off the shelf and making it mine.

For a long time we lived with an entry light fixture I referred to as the Flying Goblet light. When I was ready for something that suited us better, I turned to my idea notebook, where I had tucked a magazine photo featuring my light fixture crush: a sparkling blue glass chandelier with a $2800 price tag. Um, I don't think so. I decided to make my own chandy by embellishing something already created. Here's how:

1. At a home improvement store I found a light that was the right size and shape and had a single strand of clear crystal beads. We embellished it with extra strands of inexpensive clear and blue beads strung on fishing line and a strand of sparkly crystals we had from an old chandelier.

2. We then covered the white plastic candlesticks with strips of burlap for a rugged, imperfect look. The contrast in the fanciness of a crystal chandelier, the quirkiness of the ocean blue beads, and the homey charm of burlap suits my indecisive style!

We love our one-of-a-kind fixture inspired by a crush and created with embellishments. What can you do to make something reflect your style?

What Can You Change?

A small area like an entry still has a big impact on the ambience of your home. In the same way, small changes can lead to big results in mood and style. Anytime you think you need a grand renovation, pull back and consider what manageable step may move you forward now.

One simple way to update your entry is to refresh your front door. Our door, which I loved at one point, felt out of place as our color scheme unfolded into softer grays. We had plenty of our kitchen cabinet paint leftover (Benjamin Moore Kendall Charcoal), so we gave it a try! That small change transformed the space.

BEFORE

AFTER

Organize Your First Impression

An entry can become the dumping ground for every family member's posses-sions, from stinky gym shoes to piles of stuff you intend to take upstairs some-day. Keeping things organized in the 180-degree visual field from the front door makes a big difference in how your space feels.

Even though we have a very small coat closet in our entry, it's the only closet on this floor, and it's filled with my husband's guitars. To help reduce visual clutter, we turned to three essentials for an organized and welcoming entry:

1. Hooks

Decorative wall hooks can bring more order to your entry if you have a small coat closet or no closet at all (as in our situation). If you hang hooks in drywall, increase stability by first mounting the hooks on a piece of wood and then use wall anchors to mount the wood to the wall.

2. Landing Zones

Create a specific landing zone for the items that most frequently pile up. Once everything has a designated place, it's easier to maintain order. Decide which items cause clutter in your home and make it your mission to give them a home—or give them away!

Paper and mail are common offenders. Establish zones and actions for each category. In my home I put unnecessary flyers, mail, envelopes, or newspapers directly in a recycling bin. Bills go directly to a bill-paying basket. At the end of each week, I empty the baskets and bins so I can start fresh the next week.

3. Contained Storage

Closed storage restores visual order. My two favorite pieces in my entry are my flea market dresser and my baskets. Both give me a place to stash items we use regularly in the entry and yet keep the room from looking cluttered.

Maximize a Small Entryway

If your entry is small or nonexistent, there are decorative and functional ways to visually set apart the doorway area:

1. Add a small rug to define the floor space right by the door as your official entry.

2. Establish borders with style to outline the space. Add trim, wainscoting, wallpaper, or a pretty color to the walls surrounding the door.

3. Place small key hooks or coat hooks on the wall nearest the door. Even if they're just a few feet away, you will expand the area of the entry.

4. If you don't have room for an entry table lamp, improvise your light options! Hang a cute lantern or small candle holder with a battery operated candle on the wall nearest the door.

5. A chair or sofa facing the living space and with its back to the entry door can be a visual separator between the areas. Other options include a console table, half wall, or even something small like an umbrella stand between the door and the living space.

Take a Creative Risk

Making a bold decor move on a whim can be great fun. I knew I wanted a big glass lamp for the entryway that wouldn't be dwarfed by the stairwell or the high ceilings. Nothing I saw matched the vision in my head or my budget. So when I noticed a big blue glass water jug at a flea market, I knew that with a little bravery on my part, it could become the beautiful lamp I was dreaming of. I brought it home and proudly declared to my husband, "I'm going to make a lamp!" I never thought those words would come from my lips (nor did he). But this lamp was so easy to make that I wondered why I had never tried making one before.

You really can make a lamp from just about anything! That's great news for those of us who love unique fixtures and don't want to spend a fortune.

DIY: A Water Jug Lamp

1 Find a glass water jug (or vessel of choice).

2 Buy the lamp socket and cord at a hardware store or reuse one you already have. Lamp kits are available, but I chose individual pieces so I could have a clear cord.

3 If your cord is not pre-attached to the socket, attach the wires (consult an electrician if you do not know how to do this).

4 Set the socket in the spout of the jug and pull the electrical cord out of the spout. If you want the cord to go inside the glass, you need a special drill bit to cut glass to allow the cord to come out the side near the bottom of the bottle.

5 Use a hot glue gun or other adhesive to stabilize the socket in the jug.

6 Set a wire ring-style lampshade on the socket.

7 Plug your lamp in and pat yourself on the back because you made yourself a cool LAMP!

I'm not an electrician, so I won't tell you how to attach the wires in case my misinformation causes you permanent injury or death. Who has time for that?

Authenticity Welcomes People In

While the entry is the perfect space to create a happy first peek into the life you live and the sanctuary you love, the goal isn't to present a perfect image. You will have days when the mess overrides your desire for order. You will have weeks when your plans remain intentions and don't unfold into actions. Or, if you are like me, you will have seasons when keeping up with the pets and with the family becomes your *only* focal point!

It may take a little time and creativity to assess what TLC your entry needs, but it's a space worthy of attention, so enjoy the process! And give yourself grace along the way.

Your entryway becomes an intentional space that invites your family and guests deeper into the heart of your home.

Closer Look
{STYLE}

Defining Your Design Style

Your style can weave together a beautiful story of your life and home. These four tips can help you shape and inspire a home that will be unique to you and will help you feel more connected to where you live:

1. **Establish your home's purpose.**

   How do you want to use your home? As a place for rejuvenation? A place to unwind with family? A place to welcome new friends? Defining the purposes of your home can help you select styles that will be the most appropriate for how you will use your space.

2. **Brainstorm "inspiration words" to tell your story and create the mood of your home.**

   Draw ideas from places you love (or want to go!), the style of your home's architecture, the landscape or terrain around your home, favorite books, colors, flowers, hobbies, etc. Select a few inspiration words to paint a picture in your mind of what your home will look like. As an example, here is a list of inspiration words that inspire my home:

   Forest & Sea. Our home is located in the Pacific Northwest, literally nestled in between the forest and the sea. Our location influences the color palette and mood of our home.

   Adventure & Travel. Our life adventures have inspired a collection of compasses, ships, porthole mirrors, and other nautical elements. We adore maps, things collected from travels, quirky or unexpected elements we've discovered, and stacks of favorite books filled with photos or tales from afar.

   Timeless & Eclectic. An eclectic blend of design styles with pieces from different countries and eras inspires us. This mix brings a timeless layer of character, texture, and richness to our home.

3. Gather inspiration photos.

Look for photos in magazines that evoke the feelings you want your home to echo. For best results, find rooms that have something in common with yours, such as size or style of windows, similar layouts, comparable architectural styles, or other similarities.

Don't worry if it's a room full of expensive things you can't have. Recreating a look on a budget is fun and completely doable. Focus on a few details that are easy to reproduce, such as open shelving displays, lighting choices, color schemes, curtain styles, or fabric patterns.

4. Consider which treasures you want to collect over time.

Once you have chosen your inspiration words, you can zero in on ideas as you move forward with your projects rather than go with every style whim or buy every random trinket you see.

Making a list of the kinds of things you want in your home saves you money (no more impulse purchases to regret later) and gives you fun things to scout out at garage sales or thrift stores.

Be Inspired by Your Home's Mood

Creating a list of the moods you want your home to convey can help you select appropriate styles and avoid purchases that conflict with the feel you are shaping.

MY MOOD LIST

happy	fun
relaxed	warm
comfortable	welcoming

HOW DO YOU WANT YOUR HOME TO FEEL?

playful	creative
serene	friendly
whimsical	nostalgic
energetic	harmonious
idyllic	quirky
dignified	romantic
lighthearted	elegant

START HERE

It's helpful to eventually figure out what your style is. But free yourself from having to pigeonhole it. Instead, as you peruse magazines, Pinterest, and blogs, note your tastes and preferences. Pay attention to the ambience you long for. The creation of a home will become more enjoyable as it starts to enhance your life and authentically express your style.

The journey to your unique style is enjoyable because it always leads you home.

Mix Up Unexpectedly Great Style

I admire a look that's a mix of unexpected layers of patterns, textures, and styles all happily residing together in a space that exudes personality over predictability. This works best when the choices aren't over the top. I'm not a fan of trying really hard to "design" a room to look good or trendy. I would rather bring together awesome pieces over time and let them speak for themselves. A comfortable mix oozes personal style even if you can't put your finger on how it came to be!

Consider what mix adds up to your great style.

1. Go Global

Expand your range of decorating options and inspirations by looking at art and decor from other regions. Or seek out accessories with a global feel from secondhand and antique stores. Etsy and eBay offer handcrafted items, art, and decor from artisans and sellers all over the world.

2. Go Classic and Modern

If you lean toward a modern style, add in a classic or antique piece. Or, if you have a very traditional style, consider adding a few modern touches or reinvent your traditional look by mixing in painted and natural wood pieces.

3. Go Crazy

Embrace the unconventional if it makes you happy. Choose a color, fabric, accessory, or furniture piece that is not even in style right now (zig when everyone else is zagging!). If others think it's a crazy choice because it's too bold, too light, or too dark, embrace your choice every day because you love it regardless of what "they" say.

4. Go Bold

Big and bold choices are memorable and make a great impact. A bold pattern on a chair. A large light fixture over your table. A big, bright sofa. A huge mirror over a cabinet instead of a bunch of smaller accessories. Take a risk and be confident in the look.

2

A Place to Gather

{ Living Room and Dining Room }

Does your home offer friends and family a warm invitation from the entry area to a welcoming place to gather? For most homes, a living room is the first room we come to as we leave the entry. Whether you need space for sitting or more room for other activities your family enjoys, this space has the potential to become a purposeful, meaningful space for actual living.

Sometimes a living room is a challenge to furnish because it's more formal than our lifestyle, and so it becomes underused. Or it's difficult to define because it's fully visible from the front door and lacks a substantial entrance. Our task and goal was to figure out how to make the most of our living room. We had a family room and a TV room, so the purpose of this space was a bit of a puzzle. And its small size and narrow shape, out of proportion with its high ceiling, posed a few decorating difficulties.

Presenting another conundrum, our living room and dining room are connected. Before being defined, the living room was basically the family's

CLEAR YOUR
SPACE FOR NEW
POSSIBILITIES

CREATE AN
INVITING ROOM

DIY—DECORATE
WITH PLATES

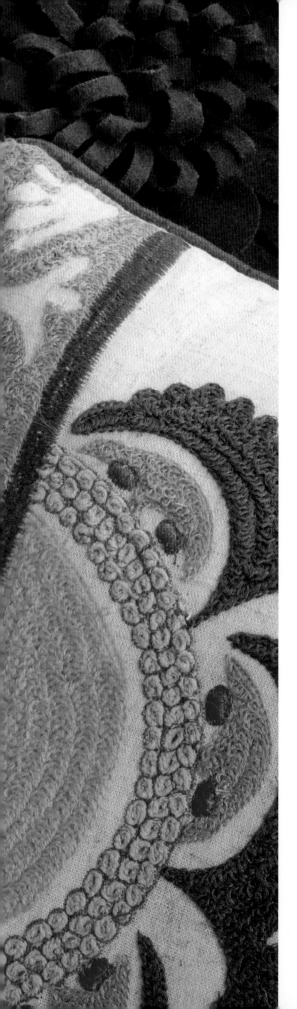

path to the dining room (and the kitchen beyond) and a dumping ground for everything from backpacks to musical instruments. I had no desire to experience a life-altering injury while stepping over random objects on my way to get my morning coffee, so solutions became a matter of personal sanity. "Serenity now" was my mantra for a long time.

Which of these situations describes a challenging space in your home?

a. small or awkwardly shaped
b. cluttered
c. undefined
d. part of a builder's vision that doesn't fit your own
e. all of the above

If you have an awkward room anywhere in your house that has been flustering, take heart. With a little thoughtful reimagining, any space can be enjoyed more fully.

An Empty Room Is Full of Possibilities

Want to know a secret to reimagining your space? When you're ready to see your awkward room from a new perspective, simply reset it back to its original state: empty.

Deciding what to keep, move, or get rid of can be hard, especially if you have things that hold emotional value or spark a little guilt when considering letting them go, but it's worth it. Donate items to worthy causes and move pieces to different rooms.

You may panic at first when wondering how to refurnish or reuse the space, but ignore that discouraging voice of fear. An open space is FREEING. Suddenly, opportunities abound. Cartwheels may ensue and impromptu dance parties are a possibility.

Empty rooms offer the hope of a room you'll love and use.

COULD YOUR ROOM BE A...

library	smaller sitting room
dining room	media room
craft area	garden room
home office	walk-in closet
mudroom	reading room
homeschool room	workout room
playroom	game room

START HERE

Think about which room in your house isn't being used as well as it could be. Explore what isn't working.

What space are you lacking in your home that you might find if you were to reimagine space you already have?

Create Your Plan

There are two essential steps to planning your room refresh:

Define the purpose of your space.

What activities will happen in this room? What function does this room serve in your home?

Choose the right furniture to accommodate that purpose and your family's needs.

Whether you repurpose what you have or start fresh, consider what pieces make sense in terms of size, scale, style, and function.

My Plan in Action

To move forward with intention in our living area, I formed a modest plan of action. We emptied the space and determined the purpose of the room to be an inviting extension of our entry and an expansion to our dining space. Next we incorporated furniture pieces that served that purpose.

Our space didn't get any bigger or fancier with our changes, but now it has a purpose that serves both rooms. Throughout the process, we selected flexible pieces we can draw closer into the room for intimate seating or pull back to create space for an additional table during large dinner parties. As a bonus, we're inspired to keep the area clutter-free and enjoy it every day.

A reader of The Inspired Room blog suggested we call our space a gathering room! Yes. That is exactly what the room needs to be called. It's been a wonderful place to relax with family and to gather friends ever since.

The empty room helped us reimagine our space.

LIVING ROOM DETAILS

1 A new cabinet provides storage and glass doors for displaying dishes and books.

2 The top is a useful surface for decor and lamps, and as a wonderful serving buffet during larger dinner parties.

3 A pair of lamps sit on the console for visual repetition and more light around the room.

4 For extra seating, we tucked upholstered footstools beneath the stairs.

5 Stools and a leather ottoman create places to prop up feet, set trays, or provide extra seating.

6 We added a deep wingback settee scaled for the size of our room. It provides the perfect place to curl up with a good book.

7 The neutral tone of the settee allows me to adorn it with seasonal pillows and throw blankets.

8 To create a cozier nook, we framed the window with soft white curtain panels.

9 We finished off the room with lighting features and special, substantial accessories.

A Dining Room That Invites You to Stay

As welcoming as you want your home to be, dining rooms in particular can end up feeling standoffishly stiff—the kind of room you only use when the boss comes over for dinner. Try thinking about this space as you would any other room in your home. Pay attention to the small details that will make the difference between a room you simply pass through and a room that invites you in daily to connect and converse over a meal.

My dreams for our dining room were simple. I wanted a room that was comfortably quirky enough to put our guests and family at ease, yet stylish enough to dress up for those special occasions when one feels inclined to whip out the crystal glasses.

Here are three essentials for an inviting dining room:

1. A Striking Statement

If you feel that your dining room lacks personality, why not start with a statement piece? A dramatic light fixture or a substantial piece of art or furniture draws attention and sets the tone for your space.

A hint of old-world charm became our unique statement. We removed a rather unoriginal chandelier and then installed an oversized outdoor copper-and-iron lantern. Instantly, this became our focal point and a design launching point.

2. A Refreshed Backdrop

Oftentimes the ideal starting point is to address the backdrop elements, such as walls and floors.

After years of living with wall-to-wall carpet (not ideal in a dining room), we celebrated the day we installed beautiful hickory hardwoods. The rustic two-toned wood transformed our space and provided a visual connection between the rooms.

At the time, this space was a sophisticated dark gray with white trim. I loved the look until the day the dining room walls begged me to be white. Don't worry. My walls don't really talk to me. And if they did, they would insist on being covered with white wood planks. But to suit our budget, we painted the drywall white instead. If I squint, I can pretend it's wood.

The cheery white backdrop and complementary flooring create a clean canvas for our ever-changing decor.

KEEPING IT REAL

Years ago we painted our table white without the leaves in place. When it came time to expand the table, we realized the leaves were still *au naturel*. We kept them that way and have ever since! Our happy accident has become a unique statement piece.

3. Sanity-Saving Storage

I function best in streamlined, organized spaces. I receive so much joy each time I open the cabinet in our dining room and actually find what I'm looking for.

If your home has limited storage, consider adding freestanding cabinets. While buying storage pieces initially felt like a splurge, the sanity-saving impact has been worth it. Not only did we introduce unique design elements, but we cut down on visual clutter. We're less likely to lose items because each storage piece has a distinct purpose. If it gets stuffed, we know it's time to pare down.

Beauty, simplicity, and function matter as much on a daily basis as they do when we welcome guests into our home. The choices we make can fulfill those three purposes.

Our rustic, beveled glass mirror reflects light and expands the room. I love how it reflects and doubles the impact of our lantern.

The hospitality cabinet is functional and adds warmth.

OPPOSITE: Our cart is ideal for serving and storage. I often keep a lidded basket on the shelf to hold extra candles or entertaining supplies.

DINING ROOM DETAILS

1 Our dining table and eclectic chairs are smaller scaled to fit the space, but their style still offers impact.

2 The copper pots and the bronze horse figures complement our light fixture, which is also our focal point, and unite the room.

3 Years ago we had curtains made from a timeless ikat fabric for one of our old houses. We loved the fabric so much we saved it for years, hoping to use it again. The curtains bring a lively pattern to a fairly neutral room.

Everyday Centerpiece Style

When I was a girl, my mom was really into decorating our tables. I was always so excited about her centerpieces at the dinner table. Now I love to do this in my home. To this day, seeing a centerpiece on my table inspires me to celebrate even ordinary days. Create your own fun focal points. Select a combination of objects that inspire you.

Put It Together

1. Pick one or more things from the list of containers and elevators.

2. Select objects to place in containers and on elevators.

3. Consider if you need fillers as a base or to finish off the look.

CONTAINERS AND ELEVATORS

- hurricanes, cloches, jars, pitchers, bottles, lanterns, vases, or terrariums

- trays, platters, baskets, bowls, wood cutting boards, crates, or wreaths

- cake plates, books, small wood boxes, or footed bowls

- candleholders for votives, tapers, or pillar candles

+

OBJECTS

- natural elements, such as pinecones, succulents, small plants, or flowers

- edible or faux fruit and veggies, such as pears, artichokes, apples, pomegranates, or lemons and limes

- candles (votives, tapers, pillars, floating, or battery operated)

- accessories, such as book pages, teacups, picture frames, mirrors, or interesting objects you love

- items to inspire the seasons, such as faux snow, acorns, cornhusks, pumpkins, ornaments, seasonal blooms, shells, or evergreen branches

+

FILLERS

- moss, sprigs of greenery, small rocks, sticks, branches, silk leaves, or flowers

- faux snow/Epsom salt, sand, or water

- embellishments, such as string, twine, ribbon, fabric, linen, or burlap

- battery-powered string lights

Creative Combination Ideas

- hurricane jar + small pebbles + water + floating candle

- stacks of books + teacups + succulents

- wood tray + pinecones + brass candlesticks + white candles

- driftwood wreath + pomegranates + sprigs of greenery

- cloche + ornaments + battery-operated string lights

- glass bowl + water + real or silk flowers

Helpful Tips

- Vary the height of the objects for a more interesting combination of elements.

- If you will be dining, a low centerpiece won't block people's view or conversation.

- Repetition of objects will make a greater impact.

- Store supplies in a convenient location so that you can decorate on a whim with ease.

Everyday on Display— Plates and More Plates

I prefer to decorate with things we actually use, so plates are a great example of everyday on display at our house. And I think the best arrangements are those that we don't overthink. For example, our white plate wall was hung one Friday night not long before guests arrived. Most people are worried about getting food to the table, but me? No, not me!

I also use vibrant blue plates on another wall for visual impact. An everyday item becomes a work of art when it's positioned for the eye to enjoy. Discover plates or platters of various styles at discount stores such as HomeGoods, garage sales, or secondhand stores.

DIY: Plate Wall

Create a fun dimensional and textural art wall with plates (or other favorite collections):

1. To be precise, trace each plate onto regular or tracing paper. Cut out the shapes and arrange on the wall using double-sided tape or poster putty until you have a layout you like. Use a finely sharpened pencil to pierce the paper and mark the wall where you want the hook and nail to go.

    Or...consider winging it! The worst that could happen is you'll end up with a few extra holes to fill. And believe me, I have a few extra holes in the wall hiding behind my plates.

2. Use standard wire and plastic plate hangers that stretch around the edges of a plate. For awkwardly sized or shaped platters, heavy objects, or pie plates, we use English plate hanging fabric disks ordered online. Dampen the fabric of the disk with water. As a paste forms, attach the disks to the back of the plate. Let dry overnight. Then hang the item with the attached hook.

3. To refresh the wall, consider mixing in decorative pie plates, small bowls, or pretty trays! There are no rules for what would be fun on a wall. Consider whatever else you love or collect!

TIP: Use a hot glue gun to affix metal pop can rings to the back of your plates for a budget-friendly hanging hook.

Simply Gathered

Our first family holiday after these rooms came together was a Thanksgiving dinner for eleven. We were excited to experience our new expandable dining space and gather the family around the table over a delicious feast. While we still only had a table for six, my girls and I set up a humble foldout utility table for added seating.

As the aroma of that Thanksgiving meal filled the room and our dogs took their hopeful places under the table, we rallied together to give thanks. The blessing of a family and a warm and comfortable home made this occasion special and memorable. Every day we are thankful that we united two rooms and created an intentional space to gather people rather than things.

Closer Look
{FURNITURE}

Every Piece of Furniture Has a Role

Furniture enhances our comfort and reflects our family's story and personality, so the details matter. Consider the mix in a room and which role each piece plays to simplify decisions and make a great impact with less stress, stuff, and money. Identify the pieces you already have and what you might add to or improve on.

 An anchoring piece catches the eye and grounds the space. Consider an antique armoire, quirky cabinet, console table, bold sofa, a substantial rug or piece of art, or even an existing feature, such as a fireplace. You might add in another later, but it's safe to start with one!

 Supporting pieces are furniture elements with the purpose of comfort, invitation, and function. They can be stylish but not showy. They may be neutral, subtle in color or pattern, or understated in style. These foundational pieces can visually balance a room with several personality pieces.

 Personality pieces offer distinct style but can serve a less prominent role than an anchoring piece. These are fun accent and functional pieces, such as unique end tables; boldly colored, patterned, or interesting chairs and ottomans; creative coffee tables; and accessories. Add a few of these for restrained impact or several to punch up the energy.

Add Furniture in Stages

An intentional, cohesive room emerges when you take time to add the right pieces for function and style.

1. Select an **anchor piece**. A great new/old/secondhand eye-catching piece will anchor your space. Search for the right piece for your budget. The thrill of the hunt is fun!

2. If you start with a simple nondescript sofa, pair it with painted or wooden end tables for function. So far, so boring? No worries. Those are your **supporting pieces**.

3. Add **personality**. Find an ottoman in a vibrant fabric that complements your sofa. Add in a stylish lamp.

What to Keep, Give Away, and Get

START HERE

While it could be fun to fill a house with new furniture in one epic shopping spree, taking your time leads to a charming, more authentic home. Look around your house and make a list of items that reflect you and your taste and that still serve you well. Does what you have work where it is, or could some pieces work better in a different room?

Now make a list of things you're ready to part with or that could use a makeover. Editing out what no longer functions well allows you to start with a fresh vision. Enjoy the adventure of acquiring pieces you love and that tell the story of your life, one chapter at a time.

Decisions, decisions! It's easy to become overwhelmed by the options. I use these four principles and questions to think objectively and creatively and to simplify choices. Walk through these topics and ask yourself the questions. An ideal piece will meet all or at least a few of these four expectations!

1. FLEXIBILITY. Could it be used in more than one way or room? Is it appropriate, durable, and practical for all members of my family to enjoy?

2. STYLE. Does it reflect my style? Is it something that makes me happy and will add character to my home?

3. PURPOSE. Is it an anchor piece or a personality piece, or will it serve in a supporting role? Does it fill an actual need in my home, or will it just add unnecessary visual clutter?

4. QUALITY. Is it something I will *keep, use,* and *love* for a long time?

Quality over Quantity

The secret to establishing a signature style on your budget is to focus on accumulating *quality* over *quantity*. I define quality furniture as something worth investing in, bringing home, and hanging on to.

- Don't let a limited budget cheapen your style. Focus on quality choices, even if that means embracing empty spaces longer while you hunt for and gather things you love. Learn ways to mix and match things you adore at various price points to complete your look for less.

- Quality doesn't necessarily mean expensive. A quality piece may be an antique table you adore because it was handed down from your grandparents. It could be a wonderful sofa you scrimped and saved for because it's the perfect color and shape. It may be an amazing cabinet you discovered on clearance at a consignment shop.

- Don't hang on to furniture that adds more visual clutter than joy. Let it go!

- Quality pieces are building blocks for your style. A quality anchor piece can define your look and bring a wonderful patina, texture, and ambience to your home as you slowly weed out or replace items that don't speak to you.

Remember, fads or flimsily constructed items will waste money and steer you in the wrong style direction.

It's great to be head over heels in love with each piece, but it's more important to love the way a room feels as a whole.

Create Fresh Arrangements

It's all in the mix! If you share your home with a spouse or family, mix in a little of each personality so your furnishings tell the whole story. Add layers with new and old furniture gathered over time from various places. Mix materials (upholstery, painted wood, metals) for character and interest.

Try a new view. While a sofa is often set against the largest blank wall in a room, it may be more interesting and better use of space to place a long cabinet or console table (your anchor piece) against the wall. Use a large area rug to ground your sofa and chairs in a conversation area near the middle of the room or gathered around a focal point, such as a fireplace or the anchor piece. You can also separate spaces with furniture (the back of a couch or a console table) and create rooms within the room.

Do what makes sense! Place a coffee table or ottoman 14 to 18 inches from a sofa and look for side tables that are 20 inches to 22 inches high. Don't spread out pieces of furniture so far in a room that people have to shout to carry on a conversation or get up to set their drink down!

TIP: When you have two tall pieces of furniture, position them across from each other for symmetry. If you have just one tall piece, balance the room with art or another statement piece across from it.

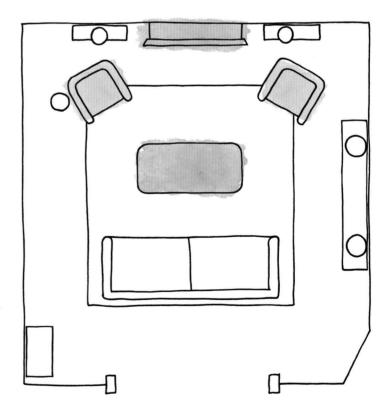

The Design Rule of Three

While some design rules might be intimidating or frustrating, the best ones give you freedom, confidence, and a formula to assess why something does or doesn't work. Symmetry, repetition, and scale help bring visual order and peace to a space.

The rule of three applies to many decisions you'll face as you arrange furniture, accessories, and even lighting. Consider how these principles for furniture could help you create pleasing rooms for conversation and real living.

- Your furniture should fill about two-thirds of your room.

- Ideally a coffee table is two-thirds as wide as your sofa.

- A room arrangement of three pieces tends to be more appealing.

- Artwork and mirrors above a sofa or bed should be about two-thirds the width of what is below.

You can take liberty with the rule of thirds! You know what they say: When you know a rule, you can break that rule. And that's okay, too! It's your home, so put it together in a way that makes you happy!

3

A Space That Nourishes

{Kitchen and Pantry}

The kitchen is the starting point for living life at home. It's where we begin many days brewing coffee, packing lunches, and discussing schedules; and its where we connect in the evenings after busy days as we make dinner (or open boxes of takeout, let's be honest).

My kitchen began its existence as a nice but fairly typical builder style. It wasn't my dream kitchen, but I was grateful it had all the basic amenities and I didn't need to update it right away with expensive appliances or features. In time I wanted to find ways to reflect my taste and to create a place of emotional connection and nourishment for our family.

It makes sense that we would want to pour our hearts into creating a hardworking, pleasant kitchen that nourishes us—a space we feel emotionally connected to. Even if your kitchen is not that place yet, don't lose hope! Whether it needs a major overhaul or just a few tweaks, it's fun to dream and consider what would transform even a humble kitchen into a room you love.

GATHER LESSONS
FROM A REMODEL

EMBELLISH—TURN
SOMETHING NEW
INTO AN ANTIQUE

ORGANIZE SHELVES
AND A PANTRY

Take Time to Live in Your Kitchen

Between all the activities, meals, and cleaning that take place in the kitchen, you can feel as if you live in that one room! By taking the time to consider the life you experience in that space, you'll notice your kitchen's challenges and be able to gather creative ideas for simple solutions.

Over time my daughters and I noted the challenges of working together in a layout suited better for a solo cook. The kitchen felt crowded and choppy because of all the things jutting into the space (cabinets and a peninsula) and hanging down (pendants and chandelier). We observed how much light came in, where the darkness settled too often, and how hard it was to reach our most-used items. And we considered what changes could make daily experiences more enjoyable.

My first change was quite small, but it brought immediate satisfaction. I simply removed a few cupboard doors to create open shelves. This instantly opened up the room, and the visible shelves filled with my collection of white dishes made the kitchen brighter and more personal without spending a dime.

A kitchen nourishes your family in many tangible and intangible ways, so improving the physical space to make it more inviting is worth considering as your budget allows.

↰ *START HERE*

For a few weeks, pay attention to how you use your kitchen and how the light, storage, and layout function or don't. What changes would inspire you to enjoy your kitchen more often?

Get Inspired

Keep your dream and steps toward it alive with a kitchen-inspiration notebook. A regular three-ring binder is a great tool to organize:

- magazine photos of favorite rooms, appliances, and colors tucked into clear sleeves

- notes about what you've done and what you'd like to do

- sketches of possible designs and layouts

- receipts, flyers, brochures, contractor business cards, and other information

As you collect images and ideas, you will begin to notice common design elements and features that can be incorporated into your own kitchen.

TIP: If you want professional advice, call in a kitchen contractor or designer to help you evaluate possibilities and costs. This is often a free consultation that can help you form a game plan.

Set Project Goals

Home dreams become realities when you know your style and start setting goals to get the look you want. Because remodels of any size can take on a life of their own, it's wise to identify goals for your space and set boundaries of where you'll call it quits.

Start by listing immediate goals you have for a kitchen improvement but don't hesitate to dream a little bigger. It can be worth the wait to save up and do several projects at once. Consider the space as a whole to decide which elements you want to splurge or save on, what part of the project you might do yourself, and what priority order makes sense for the work flow and cost. You'll spend less on updates because you'll be confident in what you really want to change.

TIP: Look at pictures of rooms you love to explore your taste. This helped me realize how much I prefer simple, classic, cozy over fussy, and contrast in color and texture.

BEFORE REMODEL:
The kitchen before the remodel was dark and too divided up for how we wanted to use it. Our goals for improvements were to lighten the space, remove obstacles, and eliminate upper cabinets.

1. Installed a new range exhaust hood

2. Added a new sink

3. Replaced counters

4. Installed a new faucet

5. Placed subway tile on wall

6. Painted cabinets and walls

7. Installed new wall sconces and ceiling light

8. Added a freestanding island

9. Added tongue-and-groove paneling

10. Removed pantry door and added shelving

11. Removed breakfast bar and added six new drawers

Embellish!

{KITCHEN ISLAND}

Nothing says charming like a well-loved antique! So why not give a brand-new piece a head start? Our kitchen island started out as a new unfinished piece, but vintage charm was just a few steps away. Choose a bland piece of wood furniture and enjoy your free therapy.

1. Use sandpaper or a hand sander to rough up the surface.

2. Get violent. Take your fancy DIY tools—a plastic lunch baggie filled with screws and nails will do the trick—and swing the bag wildly at your furniture. (Warning, sharp screws can fly out of the bag, so double bag them and wear safety goggles and gloves.)

We further personalized our island by replacing wood pegs and knobs with our favorites: brass Anthropologie animal knobs and hooks from Rejuvenation.

3. Now, things will get really ugly. Take a screwdriver and jam it into the wood a few times.

4. With a hammer, bash in the crisp new corners and edges until your piece looks as if it's been moved around the country a few times. You might want earplugs.

5. Sand the rough places so you won't get slivers, then wipe off the dust with a cloth.

6. Apply a wood stain that complements your room. With a regular paintbrush and a foam one, we applied Minwax Jacobean for a medium-to-dark tone. (Follow the product's directions.) Then wipe the excess off with a cloth and apply again. If your piece accepts the stain right away, once may be enough. The stain will settle in the distressed parts, and those areas will become darker than the rest.

7. A coat of Aqua Spar (a marine-grade varnish) will give a nice water-resistant finish.

8. Lastly, if you are painting any portions, finish with two coats of paint (we used the same color and finish of paint as our upper cabinets).

Get Organized

Open Up Display Shelves

You can make your kitchen feel more spacious with open shelves. Get the look by removing an upper cabinet door or two or by hanging attractive shelves on an open wall. Here are a few tips for styling open shelves without cluttering your kitchen:

- Group similar things together for impact.

- Only display what is visually attractive.

- With sticky tack (or plate stands) affix decorative white plates to the back of the wall of the open shelves and stack your everyday plates in front of them.

- Vary shapes and sizes for visual interest.

Clear the Space

As I mentioned before, it is helpful to remove what you don't want before you add in what you do want. We pinpointed the peninsula breakfast bar (aka the junk collector) as the main culprit for traffic flow frustrations. So when we were installing hardwood floors, I asked a contractor about the feasibility of removing that peninsula and relocating the dishwasher next to the sink.

Before I knew what hit us, out came a sledgehammer! Just as we had hoped, removing the breakfast bar peninsula opened up the room in a dramatic way.

Such drastic measures are not required to create a clean slate. Simply decluttering your space can inspire a new vision.

Increase Efficient Storage

When you reassess your stuff and consider removing or relocating items to create a clearer workspace, you also increase the efficiency of your storage spaces. Do you have a food processor or bread maker or stack of dishes you never use taking up prime cabinet real estate? What can you move or get rid of to make more room for what you actually use?

Our new, open kitchen inspired us to *increase* the amount of efficient storage. We installed six heavy-duty drawers conveniently placed just to the right of the relocated dishwasher. We also benefit from the efficiency of a small but functional kitchen island and pantry shelves.

Designate a Pantry

Every kitchen benefits from a pantry. If you don't have a separate one near the kitchen, there are still options. Designate shelves in a cabinet, add a center island with storage below, install hanging racks on the back of a door, or even employ a basket as a stand-in pantry.

Our pantry is located under our stairs. Simple changes increased its charm and accessibility.

- We removed the door to make the pantry an accessible extension of our kitchen.

- We replaced wire shelving with more stylish, functional, solid wall shelves from IKEA.

- We lined shelves with an eclectic mix of baskets and glass jars for an attractive and flexible system for organizing everything from grains to canned goods.

- We added a wood console table for extra drawers, surface area, and a homey touch.

- We embellished our console table with colorful Washi tape (decorative tape found at craft stores) and fun knobs for a touch of whimsy.

TIP: Create a baking basket filled with items such as vanilla, baking powder, and chocolate chips so everything is ready for whipping up a quick batch of cookies.

Everyday on Display—Pantry Goods

The "butler's pantry" feel enhances the charm of our kitchen and makes the overall experience of preparing meals and organizing our supplies much more efficient too. Contrary to what you may expect from an open pantry for a busy family, ours actually stays fairly orderly without much maintenance. We attribute this phenomenon to two things: We don't buy or consume a lot of packaged foods that can clutter shelves, and our organized system of baskets and jars keeps shelves looking tidy even when things *aren't* perfectly in order.

Make it Yours

Lighting

Light fixtures can add personality and style. To bring a warm, homey glow to our kitchen, we wired in new sconces to the wall on either side of our sink. This was the only wiring investment for lighting we made in the room, and it was worth it. The space is cozy at night by the glow of these Steampunk-style fixtures.

Don't let your fixtures block your view or the function of a space. We removed two pendant lights that interrupted the visual line of sight through the kitchen. And we removed a chandelier that had previously hung over a table. A new farmhouse-style fixture mounted closer to the ceiling opens the view from the kitchen to the family room and allows us to walk freely under it to use our new two-chair conversation area.

TIP: Edison bulbs (filament bulbs) provide a beautiful glow and add a vintage charm.

TIP: Easy-to-install under cabinet lighting can illuminate your counters.

TIP: In the right space, a large fixture over a center island can be a great, useful focal point.

Cabinet Hardware

1. PLAY IT SAFE IF YOU WANT. Match cabinet hardware finishes to your appliances. Vary the shapes (for example, round knobs for cupboards and bin pulls for drawers). Consider selecting two finishes that complement your kitchen. In a traditional kitchen, you may mix brushed nickel with glass finishes. You may want to match hardware to exposed hinges.

2. GET CREATIVE. Select an eclectic mix of finishes and shapes for visual interest. I used a mix of modern satin nickel bin pulls, brass and mother-of-pearl round knobs, and mercury glass square knobs. Combining metals such as silver and gold will make the kitchen feel more timeless. My island has an oil-rubbed bronze hook and two brass animal knobs (a fox and a bunny) on the drawers.

🔖 **TIP:** Select materials that are sturdy and smooth to the touch. I like to go into a store or order a few samples online to see and feel the quality of the hardware I'm considering.

3. MEASURE AND PLAN. Be sure to measure and plan carefully if you are replacing hardware with a different style. Because we chose new, wider bin pulls, we drilled new holes and filled the old. Some of our knobs came with screws that were too long for our cabinet doors, but our contractor was able to cut the screws down to the proper size.

Sinks and Counters

Single or Double Sink?

The width of a *single* basin sink feels so luxurious, and it allows room for soaking baking sheets and larger pans. For a more streamlined look than that of a typical farmhouse sink, select a smaller profiled apron front such as the one we used. This particular cast-iron sink fits in an existing cabinet with limited modifications, eliminating the expense of a custom cabinet.

Quartz Countertops

Quartz counters are strong and resistant to scratches and bacteria! There are many beautiful colors, textures, and graining options. While you can use more than one counter material in a room, for a cohesive look, use the same material on your perimeter cabinets. An island or a baking area can be a practical place to add a different counter material.

TIP: If you love the look and feel of natural stone but don't love the price tag of a slab, stone tiles can be much more affordable and give you the same benefits.

KEEPING IT REAL

Before our kitchen remodel, my girls and I decided to paint the cabinets. We sanded and used a great primer like we do when painting furniture. The next day we discovered the primer peeling off in sheets. We laughed over our DIY fail and then had professionals prep and spray the cabinets.

TIP: Draw the eye and your mood upward by having everything from the countertops up to the ceiling in lighter shades than the lower half of the visual field.

Color

Streamlining your color scheme wherever possible can really pull your look together. A kitchen with a limited background color palette will feel cleaner, brighter, and more spacious, so tie together disparate elements with a simple but coordinating color scheme.

Simple Ideas for a Refresh

- Place a wire or metal basket near your sink for hand towels.

- Keep a crock or pottery pitcher filled with utensils near your stove or baking area.

- If you have a wide windowsill, add several small potted plants for an organic pop of color.

- Add unexpected accessories to your kitchen such as small frames, lamps, and framed art.

- Collect and display pretty cookbooks to add color, interest, and inspiration.

- Add a burst of color by painting the interior of your cabinets!

- Show off colorful or patterned dishes and coffee mugs.

- Add a countertop bowl with fresh fruit for snacking and organic color.

- If your kitchen feels dreary, bring in light with plenty of white dishes and accessories.

- Hang attractive pans and cooking utensils on wall hooks to save space.

- Find a colorful or classy teakettle for your stove.

- Add decorative molding, paneling, brackets, or corbels to cabinets for architectural detail.

- Warm up a kitchen with natural accessories, such as wood bowls, baskets, and breadboards.

- Repurpose a desk, dresser, or bookshelf to use as a kitchen workspace or storage piece.

- Punch up personality with stained glass or checkerboard floors.

- Add new or vintage accessories to liven up a tired kitchen.

- Search rebuilding centers for architectural elements to add charm and character.

DIY: Refrigerator Chalkboard

I love little chalk or dry erase boards around the house to leave messages or encouraging thoughts for our family. I wanted one on my fridge, but you can't use the magnetic ones on stainless steel, so I found an easy way to create my own. This is great for leaving inspirational thoughts or notes to the family about leftovers and snacks in the fridge. Make a refrigerator chalkboard frame in four easy steps :

1   Buy adhesive chalkboard sheets.

2   Cut a chalkboard sheet to fit an old frame.

3   Stick the chalkboard on the fridge (it has a removable adhesive on the back).

4   Use Command Strips (I buy mine at Target) to stick the frame to the refrigerator door. It makes the frame completely removable. To install, follow the instructions on the Command Strip box.

Heart of the Home

Our kitchen should be a memorable backdrop for a well-lived life right down to the peaceful moment we turn out the last light to the soundtrack of the dishwasher's soft hum.

Because the kitchen is where we can fully experience all of our senses, we have the potential to create vivid and rich memories there for our families. Traditions involving this nourishing space are probably some of the most powerful. And the time spent making meals together and celebrating life in the heart of your home will be long remembered. With a little intention, we can do this simply and often.

The ambience and experience we create every day in our kitchen is an opportunity to impact those we love with a sense of home.

Closer Look

{LIGHTING}

What Lighting Does for Your Home

Good lighting impacts and improves any room. Three reasons why lighting matters:

 1. CREATES A MOOD: Lighting warms up a space and your perspective.

 2. ILLUMINATES TASK AREAS: Lighting helps you to function around the house.

 3. ADDS PERSONALITY: Lighting enhances character, style, texture, and color.

A common lighting problem is a room with only one center light that leaves the corners dark and dreary, especially at night. Beyond that primary light and natural light, additional sources can make a big difference. Let's explore various choices and styles for each of the lighting purposes.

MOOD

- table lamps
- wall sconces
- lanterns
- string lights
- candles

TASK

- pharmacy-style reading lamps
- desk lamps
- adjustable wall sconces with swing arm
- plug-in clamp lights on bookcases and beds
- under cabinet lighting

PERSONALITY

- style that suits you
- finishes for fixtures
- scale for impact

MOOD

◆ Transform your home's mood with one pair of table lamps and add in smaller lamps or floor lamps as needed.

◆ Wall sconces provide illumination higher up on the wall for great ambience. There are even plug-in sconces. String lights are inspiring. There are many choices with thin metal wire, plug-in or battery options, and warm lightbulbs for year-round sparkle.

◆ Candles are the ultimate mood-lifter. Keep votive, taper, pillar, and battery-powered candles to use on candlesticks or in lanterns, hurricane jars, and non-working fireplaces.

TASK

◈ Slim, metal, adjustable floor lamps, such as pharmacy lamps, can easily be tucked into corners. There are similar lights for walls. In my office, I have a plug-in style wall light above a chair in the corner.

◈ Desk lamps with adjustable arms shed light where you need it. When space is limited, plug-in clamp lights are good options to place on a bed, a bookshelf, or a dresser.

◈ If your kitchen is dark, under cabinet or rope lighting is excellent. We used puck-style lighting beneath cabinets in our old house for a dramatic difference.

PERSONALITY

- As able, replace standard builder lighting with something that suits you!

- Mix styles and finishes. Consider farmhouse industrial, antique/vintage, rustic, outdoor lanterns, glam, and artistic.

- Select statement lights a size or two bigger than you think you need. Mixing sizes creates more visual interest. Glass lamps can be bigger because they don't take up as much visual space and allow light to flow through them.

- Use outdoor lighting inside! For instant charm, we put up adorable outdoor lanterns on our staircase and entry walls.

- Beneath our family room art wall, we placed a pair of good-sized glass lamps to anchor and frame the vignette without taking away from the artwork focal point.

Your Best Light

Lightbulbs can change the look of your room, and you may not even realize it! Soon after we painted our family room a soft gray, we changed some lightbulbs. Instantly, our room turned light lavender. Not the goal! We realized it was the lightbulbs giving off that hue, so we made a change for the better.

I prefer warmer, softer bulbs. Lightbulbs marked "daylight" can feel sterile and are most useful in garages or storage rooms where you want maximum bright light. Or give yourself subtle light options by installing dimmers for ceiling fixtures.

Experiment with Shades

A new shade can be just the affordable touch your room needs. White or off-white shades are classic and will give you the most light in a room, but even a soft gray can be very pleasant. Black or colored shades make a dramatic statement but will emit less light.

Too many elements in a room can feel chaotic, so as you choose lighting fixtures and their shades, decide how much attention they should draw and how they can fit in seamlessly with the overall design.

START HERE

Now that we've explored the purpose and design benefits of lighting, walk around your home and notice the mood, personality, and function of your lighting. Which rooms and spaces could be transformed by different choices?

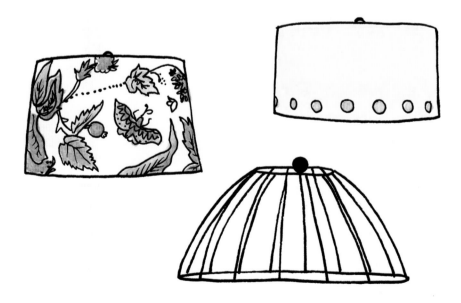

Here are a few of my favorite lighting sources: Lowe's, HomeGoods, Home Depot, Restoration Hardware, Pottery Barn, Overstock, Wayfair, Target, JC Penney, World Market, TJ Maxx, Barn Light Electric, Wisteria, and secondhand stores.

4

A Place for Conversation

{ Family Room }

We enjoy the rooms in our homes when they are set up for comfortable *living* and authentically reflect our lives. Sparsely furnished spaces or overly cluttered rooms don't draw us in because they lack the cozy incentive to curl up on a chair or put our feet up and stay awhile. If you have rooms in your house that don't draw you in, it's time to reclaim your space and start living in them!

We looked more closely at our family room when we were in the midst of transforming our kitchen with new paint and flooring. Adjoining spaces inspire one another, and it often takes that first domino to get a next step under way! Our family room is a relatively small room, but I realized this is what I loved most about it. It's not so big that two or three of us feel overwhelmed, and not so small that we can't pull chairs together to welcome others. Just right.

DIY—SHAPE A WALL
OF MEMORIES

ADD ARCHITECTURAL
DETAILS WITH EASE

DECLUTTER YOUR
FAMILY SPACES

START HERE

Look at your home spaces. Do you have an area to enjoy spending an afternoon alone that is also inviting enough to embrace friends and family for after-dinner conversation? What small changes could you make to transform a family room, study, or nook into a place to relax?

Spark Conversation

The mood we create for each room can inspire us to use it in the way we intend. Whether you have a large family room/living room or a small sitting area, how can you create a mood that will encourage conversation and relaxation? I'm all about the ambience. Best of all, ambience can be created layer by layer, over time, and on any budget.

The key to setting a mood for conversation is to arrange the furniture in such a way that people are really inspired to talk to each other and yet comfortable enough to relax and enjoy themselves in between conversations.

5 Conversation-Friendly Ideas

1. Start with the largest piece of furniture, usually your sofa, and add pieces from there.

2. Set furniture close enough together to allow for effortless conversation that won't turn into an unintentional shouting match (family peace is a good goal!).

3. Have pieces for seating at similar heights and scale so no one is sitting taller than the others.

4. Place a tray or table within reach of every seat so family and guests can easily sip a drink and nibble on a treat. Use small stools, stacks of books, or trays on ottomans as such surfaces. Our teal-blue tufted ottoman is great for gathering around a plate of appetizers with friends.

5. Make the most of large rooms. Establish more than one conversation area. Two chairs in a corner create a cozy place for a more private conversation. Lone chairs, footstools, and benches can be brought into these areas as needed.

That's Gonna Leave a Mark

When my kids were babies, we visited a friend's lovely new home with spotless white carpet. Their furniture hadn't arrived yet, so we gathered on the floor for life conversation. I was patting my daughter gently on the back, and what happened next would have been terribly awkward had anyone been a witness to it. Fortunately, a fresh baby wipe took care of the evidence. (Until today, it has been my little secret moment of shame.)

Let's face it, real humans and furry friends will leave a mark. While the potential for that increases with light, delicate furniture (or carpet), life is too short for all-brown, all-sensible furniture.

A room designed with beauty, comfort, and relaxation in mind is a way to show hospitality to yourself and to others. Consider your choices both to reflect the joy you find in personalizing your home's interior and the tolerance you have for keeping up with (or putting up with!) potential wear and tear. And most importantly, design a room intended for real living.

Everyday on Display— Real Life Within Reach

One of my favorite places to highlight everyday life treasures is on a coffee table or ottoman. In my family room, I like to group a book we're reading along with a plant or flower and an object we use, such as a magnifying glass or a pretty pen! In fact, that's my formula for any room's tablescape! You never have to go and buy fancy decor items. Celebrate what you have. Later in this chapter, see my section of ideas and tips to inspire your own tablescape groupings.

KEEPING IT REAL

I washed and bleached my white slipcovers through years of little people and puppies. But eventually, my sofa was either filthy because I rebelled against washing slipcovers daily or naked because I was tired of putting them back on. After a no-going-back stain incident with a dog (who shall remain nameless), I was done. A stylish but practical leather sofa saves my sanity.

Create a Destination

Often we're in such a rush to keep up with life that we don't take the time to simply be present in our own home. We'll be more inspired to slow down and enjoy our surroundings if we set aside a special place for ourselves and those we love.

Rather than being overwhelmed by rooms we feel we *have to* furnish and decorate, what if we thought of each area as a place we want to LIVE more fully? When we refocus our desire to create functional and inviting destinations, we're encouraged to simply use what we have and make small changes. There's no need to wait for perfect circumstances or a big decor budget.

If you are motivated to create a room that has meaning and purpose right now, then now is the ideal time to make easy changes.

- Determine your need or purpose for a destination space (personal or community).

- Add in a storage solution that suits the space and inspires you to keep it clutter-free.

- Preserve the space by making it ideal for the specific purpose. If the destination is for quiet time, have a personal lamp positioned nearby. If you need a community space, consider a center table or rug that anchors the space.

- Add in something of beauty and meaning, such as a memento from a trip or a favorite book for a private retreat area.

- Take time to transform your cozy spaces. Our family room is still evolving, yet we're motivated with every small step we've taken to create this comfortable space.

- Use your destination on a regular basis so that it becomes a habit to stop and enjoy your home.

DIY: A Memory Art Wall

Collections and art pieces give your home heart and soul and will spark conversation as they tell chapters of your story. Let your family room be a place where fun, lively, and wonderful life stories are told.

We chose sketches, drawings, and paintings from our travels to decorate our home and bring back memories of times spent together in beautiful places. These pieces have become our personalized collection and conversation starters.

1 Even if you haven't traveled far from home, use this same idea for preserving special memories close to home. I have drawings I've bought from favorite cafés, old neighborhood movie theatres, and local sights.

2 If you don't have art representing a favorite place, search for art online to add to a collection.

3 Print art you find online that is licensed for personal use, or you can purchase original art from sites such as eBay and Etsy.

Add Architectural Detail

It's the finishing details that take a room from good to great. The most charming homes have layers of character. Many have architectural personality that would exist even if all the accessories and furnishings were removed. But if that isn't your home, then it's possible to create character in permanent or even non-permanent ways by finishing the room over time with special details. We did this in various ways in the family room.

1 Our family room didn't have any ceiling trim, so we took a chance on an unconventional treatment. We had our contractor install simple flat trim (like that found along the baseboards) around the room about a foot lower than our ceiling.

2 Added wood trim, molding, stone, or tile will bring both texture and architectural detail without extensive remodeling.

3 We didn't plan to use the vast hole above the fireplace, which was intended for a TV, so we added tongue-and-groove planks as a simple backdrop for a mirror.

4 Our fireplace was originally framed with black, glitter-flecked tile. We resurfaced it with split-face, gray-and-white stacked stone and a honed, vein cut limestone tile for the hearth.

5 I change this room seasonally by adding pillows, decorating the mantel, or switching out rugs! A neutral backdrop supports my ever-changing whims.

6 Once we painted our family room a soft and warm pale gray, we were drawn into the room because of the relaxing tone.

7 We visually lowered the ceiling by painting a darker color above the molding to create the illusion of a cozier space for conversation.

8 The cabinet provides storage, and the top offers us a place to set lamps and seasonal decor. It became an anchoring piece.

Built-Ins or Freestanding Storage...That Is the Question

For years we had a big bedroom dresser in our family room to hold dishes and extra items. At the time, it served our needs. We originally had hoped to add built-ins because they can be customized to fit the space and make it feel larger. But as time went on, we had a new vision. We wanted the versatility of freestanding furniture.

When we were finally able to make a purchase, we selected a longer but more shallow piece to fit against the longest wall in the room. While it's a soft neutral, its size makes a statement! For your own spaces, evaluate whether the versatility of moveable, freestanding pieces or the made-to-fit benefit of built-ins is the right decision for your home and family's storage needs and aesthetic style.

Declutter and Add Storage

The rooms we use the most get the most cluttered. Life happens! But if we have to clear a space just to walk or sit, we won't be inspired to fully enjoy the space with our family. Keeping a room tidy isn't impossible, it's a matter of routines and habits and being intentional about what goes into the space.

Evaluate the pieces in your family room. Is something broken or threadbare or smelly? Fix it or get rid of it. Is something pretty but always in the way? Move it or let somebody else enjoy it. Are you worried about having nothing left? Remember the lesson learned from my gathering room: *An empty room is not to be feared.* It offers you clarity on what you actually need and the opportunity to invite in something you love.

To simplify your decisions, consider that every room needs some sort of storage to ease the clutter potential. So even if you don't have your dream piece yet, get creative! Find a dresser, console, desk, freestanding shelf units, or stacked lidded baskets for side tables or storage in a corner. Give each storage piece its own function and purpose to make life easier.

TIP: I wanted to avoid a rod line across the family room window which already had a lot of molding and trim detail. So I used a shortened, stationary rod on either side.

TIP: Paint can enhance existing architectural interest on a budget! In contrast to my ceiling treatment, a ceiling several shades lighter than your wall creates an illusion of a more spacious room.

Inspiring Ways to Add Detail

We've explored a few ways to enhance a room with texture and special touches. Here are more ideas to get your personal brainstorm off to a good start.

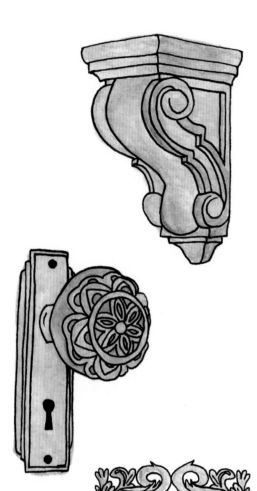

- Use paint to mimic crown molding or plaster or other wall textures.

- Add geometric wallpaper in neutral colors.

- Add corbels or brackets below cabinets or in door openings.

- Add interesting furniture with architectural detail.

- Use wood planks (rustic reclaimed wood adds character).

- Replace a newel post on your staircase with one of more unique character.

- Add ceiling medallions to period light fixtures.

- Change hollow interior doors to solid, wood-paneled doors.

- Hang salvaged architectural pieces above doorways or on walls.

- Paint builder-grade doors in gray, black, or even a color.

- Add built-ins or window seats.

- Change plastic light fixture plates to wood or metal.

- Add trim to windows and wainscoting to walls.

- Install chunkier baseboards or add additional trim to current ones.

- Add faux wood and metal tiles to ceilings.

- Change door hinges and doorknobs.

- Hang interesting or vintage picture frames and mirrors.

- Upgrade builder faucets and lights.

- Add interesting curtain rods, tie backs, shutters, and window hardware.

Embellish!
{NO-SEW LONG CURTAINS}

Finding affordable and unique long curtains isn't always easy. While you can custom-order curtain panels to suit your own window dimensions and a style you want, there's a shortcut! My goal for the family room was to simply soften the windows and add a finishing detail.

1   I found simple neutral panels at IKEA that were not quite long enough but were the color and style I wanted in our family room.

2   My mom trimmed the bottom of a pre-hemmed curtain panel I wasn't using. It was a lighter neutral that created a wonderful two-tone look when paired with the primary panels I had selected.

3   Armed with some iron-on stitch tape to avoid sewing, we attached the bottom piece of the lighter panel to the base of the IKEA curtains.

Voilà! The result is long-enough curtains with one-of-a-kind style. Score!

Simple Styling

A coffee table or an ottoman is a real focal point and an opportunity to have fun with styling! To avoid a cluttered look, keep your surface arrangement simple so it supports the room's ambience. My really easy formula is:

TRAY + BOOKS + PLANT MATERIAL + DECORATIVE OBJECT = EVERYDAY ON DISPLAY

STYLING TIPS

- Try opposites: pair smooth with rough, shiny with dull, old with new, round with square, organic with man-made.

- Make sure objects are not all too small. Choose at least one bolder item to be in focus.

- Use objects of varying heights. Books or pedestals can elevate items that seem too short.

- Remember "everyday on display"! Corral remote controls with pretty bowls or baskets.

- Fill a basket with an eclectic collection: books, fruit, artichokes, seashells, pretty buttons.

- Unify items of different shapes or textures by having them in the same color. Three various shapes of vases all in blue, for instance.

- Don't feel the need to style every table. If you have a tablescape on the coffee table, consider keeping an end table clear as a functional surface.

- Personalize tablescapes seen in magazines by using your items of similar size and shape.

- Think conversation pieces. We've used carved wood instruments and vintage game boards.

- Go simple. A tray with a few books or magazines can be a charming finishing touch.

Delight in the process. You will soon notice how the quiet, calm spaces invite you to pause and enjoy your home. And your comfortable and decluttered conversation areas will encourage you to open your home to others and share life together in a place that is, bit by bit, becoming a home you truly love.

Closer Look

{TEXTURE}

The Common Missing Ingredient

Texture is a significant (but often overlooked or underutilized) ingredient in making a home unique, attractive, and complete.

A house is most inviting when it appeals to the senses on many levels. Consider how you feel when walking through a forest or along a sandy beach. The combination of sights, sounds, and scents and the tactile experience are invigorating and soothing! The colors and patterns we select will make visual statements, but the tactile experience found in layers of texture will make a home come alive. Whether you prefer a modern, traditional, or eclectic home, the right mix of texture will contribute to whatever look you're going for.

The textures you choose can visually draw you into a space and create a complexity to the feel and look. You may be drawn to shinier, smoother textures or rustic, rough elements. Or maybe certain combinations inspire a mood you love.

When you look at your rooms and some feel cozier, there is a good chance that you have added texture to those spaces. Take your cues from your favorite rooms or from images in magazines to pinpoint the textures that suit you best.

We'll explore six ways to create a visual and tactile experience in your home that add interest, not clutter.

> *Texture is not only an ingredient in your decorating mix, it is an invitation to others to experience and enjoy a room.*

1. Rugs

Whether you prefer the simplicity of a neutral rug or the liveliness of a colorful one, rugs add texture. The organic dimension of natural jute, a beautiful wool or silk, or a faux fur or animal skin rug can bring extra beauty to a room.

Layer rugs over carpet or other rugs too, or decide to forgo them altogether if you already have beautiful wood or tile floors that bring texture to the room.

2. Accessories

Opposites attract. Add contrasting elements until you love the mix! For interest, combine smooth with rugged or shiny with dull.

Incorporate glass with dishes, lamps, or bottles; add shine with mirrors and metals; weave in natural textures, such as stones, sticks, plants, antlers, wood, or shells; and layer rugged textures, such as baskets and woven trays.

TIP: Rustic textures, such as wood, bring warmth but can add weight to a room. Balance with the light and coolness of glass or metallic accents.

TIP: If bold colors or patterns are not your style, focus on adding layers of textural elements (accessories and textiles) instead!

TIP: Scout out thrift shops or galleries for more textural works of art, including original oil or watercolor paintings rather than prints.

3. Furniture Finishes

Have a mix of furniture finishes to suit your preferred style. For a fun mix, try a variety of wood pieces, rattan and wicker, painted furniture, upholstered pieces, and shiny or metallic items.

Pair antiques with modern pieces, or use different textures on the same piece! Try fun metallic or sparkly pulls on an antique wood dresser. Add textural details, such as metal nailhead trim.

4. Fabrics

Incorporate fabrics that make you want to reach out and touch them, such as textural throw pillows, blankets, and lush bedding.

Find your favorites. Consider tweed, velvet, leather, linen, silk, fur, chenille, cashmere, cotton, burlap, crewel, mohair, and knit. Add more textural details with tufting or pintucking.

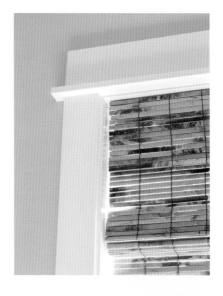  

5. Window Treatments

Consider adding flowing drapery fabrics, texture on blinds, soft Roman shades or sheers, or the chunkiness of plantation shutters.

Beautiful windows with amazing trim and an equally amazing view can be left undressed, but most windows can benefit from a little added texture!

6. Architecture

Cabinet hardware and lighting choices incorporate a variety of enjoyable texture.

Add a splash of interest to your walls with wallpaper, paint treatments, chair rails, wood wainscoting, paneling, or board and batten. Other textures can be present in countertops, flooring, tile, and stone.

We added charm and texture by installing wood tongue-and-groove wainscoting in key places throughout our home for a little bit of that old-house character we love.

Contrast Adds Beauty

If nothing surprises people in a house, it can look staged, stuck in a time warp, or not authentic. If a room feels void of texture, create inspirational variety with simple changes:

- Add in a natural wood element in a house full of painted furniture.

- Greenery in the form of plants can be a nice soft contrast to hard surfaces.

- Enrich a room that has too much softness with a basket, shell, piece of wood, or a natural fiber rug.

- Brighten a dark room with a light-toned quilt, table runner, glass accessories, or a creamy porcelain pitcher or vase.

You'll more greatly appreciate the things you already have when they play off contrast. Soon your family and guests will be drawn into your spaces without realizing that texture has extended a great invitation to them.

START HERE

Of the various textures we've explored, note those that evoke the mood you want. Now stand in the doorway of each of your rooms. Is there a pleasant mix of those textural elements? Or is there an absence or clash of patterns and color? Remove anything overwhelming and then shop around your house for the newly identified textures you love.

5

A Room to Refresh

{Bedrooms and Bathrooms}

A bedroom is a sacred space. It's the inner sanctuary of the home, where we should be able to quiet the outside voices and reset our minds and hearts on what matters most. We need a place to take a deep breath, symbolically inhaling and exhaling the cares of the day.

For many, the goal of furnishing and decorating bedrooms is probably near the end of an already overwhelming to-do list. When time and money are limited, we tend to give priority to our public areas and unintentionally delay the care of our personal rooms. But creating the order and beauty our soul craves is important.

The payoff of intentional effort and attention is the creation of a comfortable, inviting retreat, where we can shed the expectations we face during our working hours. In the quiet, we can relax and remember who we are as our truest self. When we create a place to reconnect with what and who matters most to us, we can recharge. That peace and renewal is a gift not only to ourselves but to those we love.

CREATE SANCTUARIES
FOR YOU, FAMILY,
AND GUESTS

PERSONALIZE SPACES
FOR KIDS AND TEENS

EMBELLISH—ADD
BED-AND-BREAKFAST
CHARM

The Beauty of a Bedroom

During our waking hours, we juggle schedules and scurry to meet demands as best we can. At the end of the day, we collapse exhausted, only to start all over again the next morning. No wonder our souls seem to cry out for a refuge! Our bedroom can be this kind of place for us. It can restore our sense of balance and beauty.

Does your master bedroom reset you to a more peaceful state? Or are you likely to be overwhelmed by it? Devoting a few quiet moments to a brief cleanup routine in the morning and again in the evening can create a better order and rhythm for your life. Even on those days when you awaken to a small person breathing one inch from your face saying they are hungry (these are precious moments of life!), a clean-enough and pretty bedroom can reset your mindset and day. It's the difference between starting a day with a smile or the desire to pull the covers over your head (and hope no one notices your absence).

No matter what season of life you are in, embrace gratitude and reclaim an orderly sense of your home, your schedule, and your places of beauty.

Our Haven at Home

My bedroom (that I share with my husband!) has evolved over time to be that place we can retreat to at the end of every day to find the inspiration and motivation to begin even the craziest weeks. We have a smallish master bedroom filled with a mix of new and old furniture gathered or inherited over time. Our room isn't fancy or luxurious, but it's our haven.

A pretty bedroom reminds me daily that this space is a gift. It's a place to nurture beauty in our life and find comfort and peace. It's a psychological thing for me, but seeing the pretty room I've invested myself in works to keep me in a rhythm of daily home-keeping, and in turn that rhythm inspires my day. Consider each of your changes, improvements, and times of tidying your bedroom and other rituals of refreshment as gifts you give yourself.

Slow-Decorating a Room You'll Love

Just like everyone else, my family has its times of order and chaos. But in each house my husband and I have lived in, we made it a priority to gradually and intentionally create a space that would offer us refreshment. Through the ups and downs, for better or worse, we've held tight to our dreams of a beautiful room to welcome us at the end of a long day.

While it might be wonderful to have a designer take over so we could arrive home one day to a perfectly gorgeous boutique hotel suite right there where our average bedroom used to be, the reality is that there's value in slowly decorating a room. When we take time to reflect on our style and invest our heart into a space we use daily, we feel a greater connection to it. Practically speaking, we need time to notice what causes us to feel frazzled as we start and end each day and, conversely, what small details could bring us more peace.

START HERE

We can forget to pay attention to the rooms we use daily. Try my super scientific method for noticing how your rooms look and feel.

Step One: Walk down the hall nonchalantly gazing at nothing in particular.

Step Two: As you pass by a room, do a *quick double take* back at the space in question.

Step Three: Are you inspired by what you see? If so, yay! But if you say "meh" and crinkle your nose, it's time to rearrange, reorder, or refresh immediately.

Repeat steps one through three. Brilliant, I say!

Even the small changes we make over time can result in a room that enriches our lives.

MASTER BEDROOM DETAILS

1 We make the bed with European shams and decorative pillows in soothing colors and patterns.

2 Our nightstands and cabinets offer ample storage to hide away everything we need while limiting clutter.

3 We have layers of comfortable linens and fluffy pillows for propping ourselves up to read and to enjoy occasional lazy mornings.

4 The geometric patterns on our mirror and dresser enliven the space but don't overwhelm it.

5 Displays of collected art, photos, mementos, and verses offer us daily reminders of our story.

KEEPING IT REAL

Before we bought curtains for our bedroom, we had towels on our window for an embarrassingly long time.

Bed-and-Breakfast Getaway

Imagine a hotel you (and your spouse) think would be the most restful, romantic environment for a weekend getaway. Where would you LOVE to go? What would the space look like? You can take design cues from that dream vacation getaway and pull together elements to recreate a similar feeling in your home. Here are easy ways to create a relaxing everyday getaway.

1. Refresh.

If your room is overrun by toys, electronics, and laundry, you'll never relax. Before day's end, take a big box or laundry basket, gather up the stray stuff, and set it elsewhere. While you'll have to deal with it later, at least your room will be clear enough to unwind. Dust and vacuum your room so you can breathe easy.

2. Treat yourself to quality.

You use your bedding daily, so go with quality. I prefer one set of nice sheets rather than a bunch of scratchy sheets I dread using.

3. Add layers.

When I picture a quaint B & B, I see layers of warmth. Curtains with bamboo shades or shutters underneath. Big pillow shams, pretty bed skirts, and a cozy throw over a chair. Create a warm nest and bring cozy back into your life.

4. Let there be peace.

Allow your bedroom to be a place of softness and stillness. Lots of fabric and rugs will invite you to nestle in. If you have a TV, place it in a cupboard or someplace inconspicuous.

5. Indulge your senses.

Your full experience is shaped by your senses, so pay attention to the scent of the room, the feel of the fabrics, and the choice of colors. I use a scented linen spray to freshen up sheets and the room.

6. Savor breakfast in bed.

Look for an affordable breakfast-in-bed tray. If you are planning a special "B & B night" with your hubby, place muffins and big coffee mugs on a tray and set your coffeemaker to turn on in the morning so you'll wake up to the great aroma!

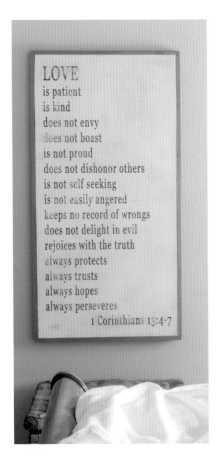

A display of verses about love from First Corinthians is one of our favorites.

🔖 **TIP:** A large lidded basket is an attractive storage spot for stowing away sleeping pillows during the day.

Shape Your Sanctuary

Transform your bedroom into a personal retreat. Consider what to let go of and what you can add to shape a sanctuary that draws you in, prepares you for rest each evening, and greets you with a pleasant feel and look each morning. After a day of all that life can serve up, you deserve a place to unwind and to restore physically, spiritually, and mentally. What ideas from this list might help you preserve your shelter from the storms and surprises of life?

- Remove as many things from the room as you can to create a peaceful space.

- Use a bedside table at least as high as your mattress if not slightly higher.

- Good reading lights are a must for ambience and nighttime reading.

- Keep electric clocks and cell phones and their electromagnetic radiation away from the bed.

- Use covered boxes, baskets with lids, or drawers to hide necessities.

- Install dimmers and three-way switches to add mood lighting.

- Give your room a good cleaning often. You'll thank yourself.

- Make your bed in the morning. All day you'll be glad you took the time.

- Avoid using your bedroom as a dumping ground for stuff. Treat your room as a sanctuary.

- Keep a notepad and pen by the bed to jot down ideas or to-do lists that could keep you awake.

- For your best night's sleep, make sure you cannot see any light from your bed.

- Avoid bill-paying areas or work zones in the bedroom whenever possible.

- Keep lightweight coverlets or blankets nearby so you can add layers as needed.

- Select two Euro-style pillows for a queen (26" x 26" square shams filled with firm pillows) and three for a king to perfectly prop yourself up for nighttime reading.

A Creative Room for Kids

Each bedroom in the home should meet the needs and reflect the style of its inhabitants. If you have children, their rooms will be their world, so it's important to create a place that inspires them as they grow and change. Children's rooms are the one place in a home where their own personalities can shine brightly, so give them an opportunity to make good design choices!

I always gave my children decorating choices I could live with, so their rooms were tasteful but still reflected their own personality. Too many options can be overwhelming for a child, so simplifying to two or three good choices empowers them to be decisive. I believe this approach taught each of my children appreciation for good design, encouraged their own artistic ability, and gave them a sense of ownership and pride in their rooms.

Teen Spaces

When our son, Luke, turned 13, he expressed a desire for a redesigned room. He was growing out of his childhood bunk bed and wanted a desk that would accommodate his current needs and interests. I wanted to give him a space that would be more reflective of who he is and a room he would enjoy and feel comfortable in, so we redesigned the tiny area with his ideas in mind.

When I start to think (and cry!) about how few years we have left with him at home, I'm happy that we took the time to create a memorable room.

START HERE

Let your teen search online and in magazines for furniture, colors, accessories, and general room designs he or she might like. Invite them to create a mood board to help guide the decorating process. Incorporate personal elements and special photos so the space becomes meaningful to them and a reflection of what they love.

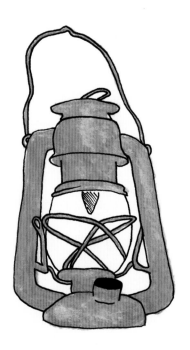

TEEN ROOM DETAILS

1 An open shelf above the gallery wall displays items from a scavenger hunt Luke did with the family as a child. He loves having the freedom to put whatever he wants on the shelves or in the frames.

2 We created a cozy corner nook with a corduroy wingback style bed.

3 A wall sconce saves space while providing light for nighttime reading.

4 For vibrant contrast and style, we placed a Pottery Barn indoor-outdoor rug in a tribal print on top of the carpet.

5 We gave an old dresser new life by adding knobs with a compass design and a fresh coat of paint to the drawers.

6 We added a deer hook for hanging favorite sweatshirts and artwork with a favorite verse.

7 One of my son's most-requested items for his room was a desk. He chose a great counter-height desk with plenty of storage and display potential.

8 A birch branch became the perfect curtain rod for the closet.

9 The slim, three-level cart serves as an ideal nightstand for bedside essentials.

6 Sanity Savers for Kids' Spaces

Don't become overwhelmed with all the cute and clever items available for kids' rooms. Start with the basics and then add layers and extra, personal touches.

1. Keep the shell of the room and foundational elements simple, neutral, and timeless so the room can grow with your child.

2. Use decorative rugs, lamps, bedding, and shelves as opportunities to show their personality and display their colorful toys and treasures.

3. Provide easy ways for your child to express their creativity and feature their drawings and art. Designate plenty of space for their ever-changing art galleries and mementos.

4. Include kids in the decorating process so they can take ownership of the space and design a room they will love.

5. Stay organized! Chalkboards, magnetic boards, and clipboards are great for artwork, and you can use them to help children learn to organize their own lists, chores, or daily schedules.

6. Make functional storage accessible. Age-appropriate organizational systems and daily cleanup times help teach children the value of maintaining order.

Everyday on Display—Mementos

Luke has a space on his wall where he displays movie tickets and other mementos from guy nights with Dad. Consider featuring awards, ticket stubs, vacation photos, notes, sporting event programs, and anything else that represents a special moment or interest in a kid's life.

A Gracious Guest Bedroom

Bedrooms can become evolving reflections of a growing and changing family, often having to serve more than one purpose in a week. In our home, our middle daughter Courtney's room is both her bedroom and the as-needed guest space. A double-duty guest bedroom serves visiting friends or family well with simple, pampering touches to make anyone feel as though they are on a special getaway.

This room also serves as a makeshift home office and library. We cram a lot of function into this small bedroom! The three shelving units came from Target. By pulling them close together, they offer the illusion of a built-in library.

The wall of curtains behind the bed inspires the feeling of a cozy cocoon and creates dramatic impact.

Special Extras for Guests

After you clean, dust, and vacuum, consider adding these eight simple touches to create a welcoming guest room:

1. A minimum of two bed pillows per guest

2. Fresh linens and an extra blanket

3. A bouquet of flowers or bud vase with a single bloom

4. Space in a closet or chest of drawers

5. A lamp and small clock near the bed

6. A welcome basket with a water bottle, a few small snack bars, a notepad and pen, an assortment of local postcards, and sightseeing brochures

7. Reading material, such as stacks of books and magazines

8. Bathing essentials (new soap and toothbrush, toothpaste, shampoo, disposable razor, bath towel, hand towel, and wash cloth)

7 Guest Room Refreshers

1. Repurpose what you have. We used an old sewing table featuring a funky teal machine as a unique nightstand.

2. Invest in a new set of lamps or lampshades.

3. Layer a rug on top of your carpet or hardwood floors.

4. Add a statement piece to be your bedroom's new focal point: a large or full-length mirror, pretty clock, piece of art, repurposed window frame, etc.

5. Use artwork to pull together a color scheme.

6. Mix in two to four new drapery panels to what you already have for a fuller look and more texture or color.

7. Add a hypoallergenic feather topper to the mattress for luxurious comfort.

TIP: Turn a small window into a grand statement! We extended the curtain rods and curtain panels clear to the walls to create the illusion of a larger window.

Embellish!
{B & B DOORS}

Don't laugh, but I've always been obsessed with the idea of creating my upstairs hallway and bedrooms to feel like a bed-and-breakfast. I picture opening the guest room doors to find a big cozy bed, piles of pillows, a bathroom with fluffy towels, delicious smelling soaps, and a stack of mystery novels by the bathtub.

To take the step toward that dream, I now have four numbered guest rooms (okay, well, they are all occupied by family right now, but they are still private retreats!). Yes, I have boring, standard, builder doors, but at least I can make them fancy with a vinyl decal, right?

KEEPING IT REAL

As much as I love a beautiful bathroom, the master bathroom in our house has been patiently waiting years for its first touch of personality. It's next on my to-do list. Really.

Bathrooms

A bathroom in one of my childhood homes was adorned with a beautiful, large chandelier. It wasn't an otherwise fancy bathroom, but I thought to myself that someday I too would have a crystal chandelier in a bathroom. I was *that* child who would ask to use the restroom in a fancy restaurant just to see if it was pretty.

While classy bathrooms with marble counters, gorgeous faucets, and beautiful tile make my heart beat a little faster, above all else clean bathrooms are my favorite. I'll admit I was also that child who wouldn't use a restroom if it smelled bad or looked grungy. (Who am I fooling? That's true today!) Tidy and fresh bathrooms boasting a little charm are a winning combination.

In our home, we have three fairly ordinary bathrooms: a master bathroom, a kids' bathroom, and a powder room. This is actually the first home we've ever had with a designated powder room on the main floor, so we feel we're living the high life even without the fancy fixtures.

TIP: Bathroom accessories, such as cotton swabs, can feel extra luxurious when they are in a fancy jar.

🔖 **TIP:** Numbered hooks give each family member and guest a designated spot for their towel.

🔖 **TIP:** Set a fluffy bath rug by the sink to keep your toes cozy and more absorbent rugs by the shower so you don't slip on your way out.

🔖 **TIP:** If you have the space, consider adding a pretty stool to your bathroom. It's the perfect spot to perch while putting on shoes or an extra space to stack towels.

DIY: Faux-Tin Tile Backsplash

If you're looking for a way to do a simple makeover for the counter area, replacing the Formica backsplash with faux tin ceiling tile is definitely worth a try. We placed ours with adhesive tape and matching trim. It looks great, adds personality, and has stood the test of time...in a boy's bathroom!

Visit TheInspiredRoom.net for a full DIY tutorial.

10 Ways to Prettify a Bathroom on a Budget

I'm always happier when I make an average bathroom at least *a little prettier than it was*. I know. For a girl who dreamed of crystal chandeliers in bathrooms, I really have lowered my expectations! It doesn't take a big budget to add personality and style to a bathroom.

1. Add a dimmer switch.

2. Hang new towel hooks.

3. Change drawer pulls.

4. Update lighting.

5. Hang quirky art and frames.

6. Add a plant or a vase of flowers.

7. Add a stylish mirror or hamper.

8. Freshen up the paint color.

9. Bring in new towels.

10. Update the backsplash.

Closer Look
{COLOR AND PATTERN}

Layers of Beauty

I am creatively energized by contrast, pattern, and color, and I love to be surrounded by things that inspire me, but I become overwhelmed if my eyes have no place to rest. Our lives can be plenty busy (and crazy), so most of us crave a peaceful home. Is that possible if you favor color and pattern? Yes! The key is to be intentional with your choices and take the time to layer, rearrange, and play with options to find the combinations that form a sanctuary for you and your family.

Color

Colors matter! I had a mood crisis when we bought our new house because all the walls were painted a dull, pinkish-beige color I referred to as "swine" on my blog. That particular shade of beige made my home feel uninviting and dingy to me. If you are ready to change your homes' colors, bring in accent hues, or showcase colors with accessories and statement pieces, this Closer Look can help you embrace a palette that welcomes and inspires.

Pattern

If each space is shouting for you to look at it, you eventually will avoid the room. But if you introduce pattern in tones and pairings that suit your personal taste, the spaces will add so much joy and richness to your home. They will complement your style rather than distract from it. If you preserve some more serene and visually clutter-free areas, you will balance out those that are more vibrant and varied.

Delight in the discovery of new colors and patterns. When browsing at antique or home furnishings stores, take photos of any appealing designs, tones, or combinations. And take pictures of your furniture, accessories, and wall tones so that when you stumble upon a potentially great addition, you can evaluate if the item complements what you already have.

With a little practice and brave experimentation, color and pattern will enhance your home and be a welcome reflection of your own personality.

A Pretty Palette

START HERE

Create a pleasing mood with color and pattern by picturing a place you love to go (or would like to go) for a getaway and use that as inspiration. What about your happy place looks and *feels right*? This can get you going in the right direction.

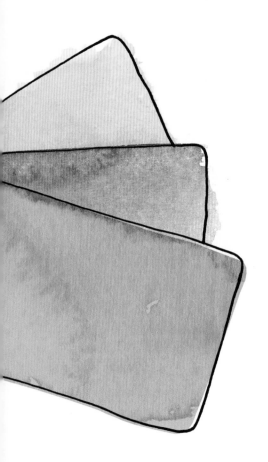

- All colors don't have to match exactly. In fact, that can be more interesting. Choose various shades and tones of complementary colors.

- In a room with little natural light, add contrast between light and dark colors.

- You can mix shades of whites and creams. A variety gives a "collected over time" look.

- A white room can appear unfinished unless accented with textures or color. It can also accentuate clutter, so a lack of chaos is essential.

- All of your rooms don't need to match in order to flow. I like variations from subtle to dramatic (such as the vibrant blue walls of my office).

- For a small space, paint walls and trim in similar shades to blur the architectural boundaries, making a room feel larger and more cohesive.

- Add white to a darker paint color used in one room to create a new complementary color for an adjoining room. Mix the exact same paint brand and sheen of paint to ensure the paint goes on smoothly and evenly when mixed together.

- Introduce trend or seasonal colors through accessories rather than with your entire backdrop.

- Use the rule of three: Repeat a color in at least three things around the room.

- If you group objects of similar color, use a variety of textures for visual interest and impact.

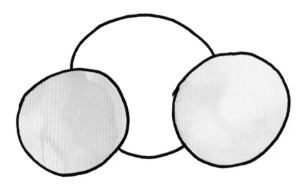

To design a palette for my office, I imagined a place that inspired me: a Four Seasons hotel in Hawaii my husband and I stayed in years ago. This whimsical curtain fabric echoes the palette of paradise and sparks happy memories.

Choose Your Best Paint Color

These questions and steps can help ensure that you love your color choice.

What in your room could inspire your paint color?

Paint colors should generally be chosen last so they can complement the design of the room.

Do you prefer warmer or cooler tones?

Warm tones can feel cozy and welcoming. Cool tones are refreshing and serene. There are warm and cool undertones for all colors, so select a tone that feels right to you.

Choose your swatches.

After you know your preferences, go to a paint store to look at swatches in the color families that make the most sense. Take the swatches outside to compare in natural light.

Try it at home.

Bring swatches home and tape them on the walls to observe them in the light throughout a day. Hold up fabrics and pillows to see which tones work best with your swatches. Even neutrals and whites can change their appearance when paired with flooring or furnishings. Pick your favorites and buy small paint samples. Paint these directly on the walls and evaluate over several days in all light. Choose your winner!

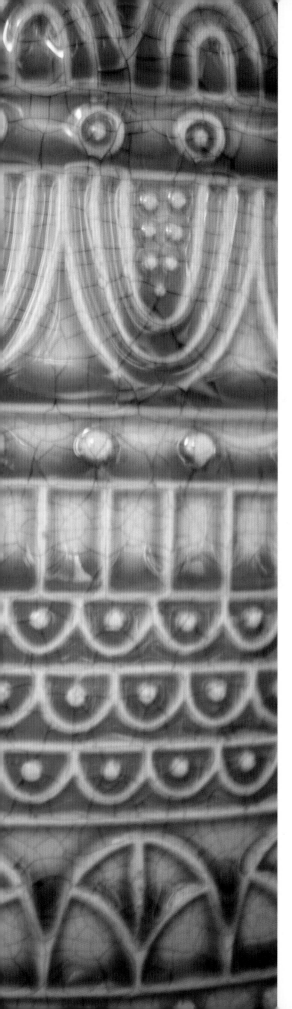

How to Mix Patterns

There are many ways to effectively mix patterns. Consider starting with a limited color palette (such as one color plus white) in patterns of various scales. These tips can help you mix, match, and experiment.

- Two similar patterns will look best together when connected by a common color or tone of color.

- You can combine three or more patterns in a room.

- Start simply! Choose a large-scale pattern and a small-scale pattern in the same color family. Mix in solids.

- You can use more than one stripe. Just make sure one stripe is wide and one is narrow.

- Use a neutral on walls and flooring to unite the patterns in the room.

- Add interesting patterns with art or objects in a neutral room for a pleasing balance.

- Wood grains and stone contribute organic pattern to a room.

Generally, it's safer to mix patterns in similar styles (traditional with traditional or contemporary with contemporary.) But there will be times when you want to be a bit more bold. Consider some of the fun pairings in the Pattern Play illustration, and give yourself permission to experiment.

Pattern Play

Buffalo Check & Small Floral

Gingham & Floral

Stripes & Tiny Polka Dots

Leopard & Stripes

Pinstripes & Large Plaid

Floral & Stripes

Small Polka Dot, Wide Stripes & Floral

Stripes & Ikat

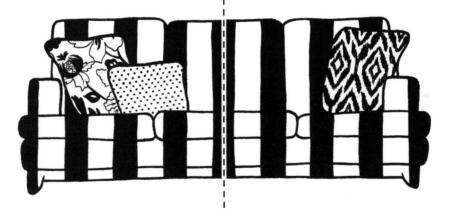

Floral, Damask & Stripes

Gingham & Botanical

Two Geometrics & Stripes

Geometric, Stripes & Toile

Stripes, Floral & Houndstooth

Geometric & Floral

6 Ways to Balance Pattern

Intentional decorating leads to a look that is cohesive and pleasing to your eye. Whether you have too much pattern or none at all, the starting place is the same: Create visual balance in the room.

1. Keep "white space" in a calming proportion to the color and pattern.

2. Consider choosing your walls, curtains, or larger pieces of furniture to be the neutrals, allowing you to add lively colors and patterns to the room without becoming overwhelmed.

3. A different way to achieve calm is to designate several solid, neutral, or clutter-free areas of a room so you can focus on a few lively focal points.

4. Distribute pattern around the room for visual balance.

5. Busy patterns can add energy and life to a room, while simple patterns can create calm.

6. To keep a room from feeling chaotic or trendy, select just one bold, new, or fun pattern.

6

A Functional Space

{Home Office and Small Areas}

Function helps us feel comfortable at home, and style helps us to enjoy keeping a home tidy and organized! If you can infuse both function and style into all the nooks and crannies of your home, you'll love where you live.

Every once in a while I catch myself dreaming of how a different house would serve our needs better. I imagine that my house is too small and I need a mudroom. An exercise room. A craft studio. But do I really *need* a new house with all of those rooms? Nah. I just need to better use the space we have. Dreaming can result in the nudge to downsize and declutter.

The good news is that you don't have to have a lot of square feet to have a functional house. The key is to utilize the space you do have to its fullest potential and give it a dose of personality too.

I've been on a several-year mission to create style and function in all spaces of my home, from my home office to the TV room to the laundry room. While I'm far from finished, I find the process to be fun.

ORGANIZE A PLACE TO
WORK AND DREAM

DIY—PAINT STRIPES
LIKE A PRO

GIVE SMALL SPACES
A BIG MAKEOVER

A Space to Work and Dream

I think everyone should have at least one small corner of their home set aside for working, dreaming, or creating. Even if it's a dining table or nook that has to serve more than one purpose, it can become *your* place when you need it.

Throughout our home we have several spaces designated as mini offices and creative destinations. A chest with a pull-down desk in our bedroom is a perfect letter-writing space. Bookshelves along the wall in our guest room double as home office storage. The TV room also serves as my husband's home office (thanks to a coffee table for a laptop and bookcases for files!).

My office is one of my favorite rooms. It's where I write The Inspired Room blog and where I conduct the related business every day. My work involves two seemingly opposite daily functions: creativity and business. It also involves super glamorous aspects too, such as taxes, spreadsheets, and sitting at a computer for hours on end! So I need this small room to inspire me and to function well for a growing business.

While the kitchen might be the heart of the home for the family, there are many days when my office is the heart *and* home for my passion.

Organizing a Home Office

I'm not a naturally organized person, but I do crave a measure of order because without it I'm likely to be a stressed-out disaster. I stumbled into my business bliss, and each new way the blog grows is a happy surprise. In order to sustain my expanding responsibilities and new life adventures, I've had to create a space where I can breathe, dream, and work.

My office has a combination of furniture pieces that offers order and beauty. The desk I bought when I first started my business eight years ago still serves me well. And while built-ins would be amazing in the small space, I love the eclectic look and the fun of collecting furniture over time. Wherever you carve out your work space, include furniture and accessories that serve and support you and your dreams.

OUR
HOMES SHOULD
inspire us
TO GO OUT
INTO THE WORLD
TO DO GREAT THINGS
& THEN *welcome* US BACK
FOR
refreshment

thrill of the hunt

1 My desk is paired with a secondhand antique secretary and a painted white hutch, where I store paint swatches, special books, computer and camera gadgets, and a variety of fun things.

2 We often use the pull-down desk part as a secondary surface for a laptop or to serve snacks!

3 The rattan shelving unit I found at a flea market is a favorite of mine. It holds notebooks, files, photos, and magazines, and it adds wonderful texture to the office.

4 To organize office and craft supplies, art prints, and other smaller items, we selected a flat drawer system to keep from losing things in the depths of deep drawers.

5 Linen boards are used for inspiration.

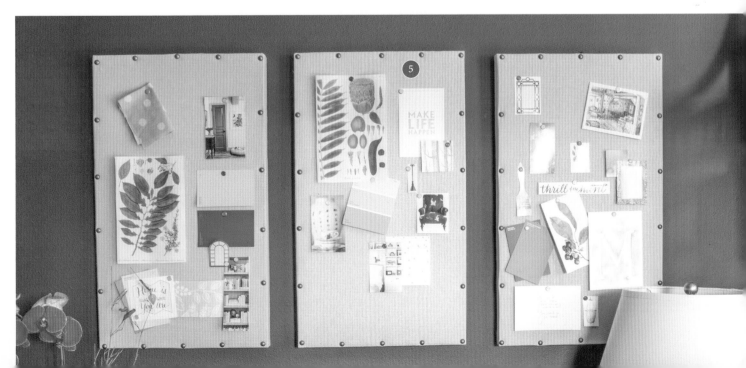

TIDY OFFICE TIPS

1. Create stations for your task items, such as paper and mail, technology, craft or scrapbooking supplies, etc.

2. Establish a place (chalkboard, dry erase board, etc.) to write your to-do lists, reminders, or inspiring encouragements.

3. File drawers on wheels let you file anywhere with ease. Also consider using portable banker boxes or crates for organizing files.

4. Consider over-the-door file holders and add tall shelves for storage that won't trip you up.

5. If you are keeping home files and business files in your office, separate them by colors or styles of container (baskets or metal, for example).

6. Give yourself some clear space on your desk, shelving, or walls so that you feel the breathing room and inspiration of "white space."

7. Motivate yourself by taking a before picture of your office and then plan a timed-session to clean and then take an after shot. Progress inspires!

8. Clear off your desk, wipe it down, and then add back only the things you really use and need.

9. Bring in your favorite mug, tea bags, and a teapot or coffeemaker to set on your shelf or side table for an inspiring beverage break.

Shaping a Multipurpose Room

If any room in our house has to serve multiple purposes, it would be this room. While the main purpose of this room is a place to gather family and friends to enjoy movies together, it also serves as an overflow guest space and my husband's home office. That's a lot for one room to handle! The secret to its success required some strategic planning. Again, in this space, built-ins would be a wonderful space-saving addition, but short of the ideal, we've made freestanding furniture work for us.

MEDIA ROOM DETAILS

1 The sectional maximizes the available seating and floor space and has a pull-out bed for guests. Too many different pieces of furniture can look awkward and crowded in a small space.

2 If you don't have room for side tables and lamps, add sconces to bring light around the room.

3 Our oversized clock is a quirky focal point that also serves a function.

④ Bookcases offer plenty of storage space. This unique piece was selected to add interest and movement to the otherwise boxy corner.

⑤ The stripes add a little pizazz, helping to unify a wall of mismatched pieces.

⑥ We repainted and repurposed an old desk to become our media stand. It's the perfect height and adds storage for game controllers and other odds and ends.

DIY: Painted Horizontal Stripes

1. Paint your wall whatever color you want to use for the base color (which becomes one of the two stripes). Make sure that the base color is different from your ceiling, baseboard, or trim color. In my case, I used Studio Taupe from Behr All-in-One in a flat finish.

2. Measure the height of the wall and divide by an odd number to set the size and number of your stripes and to ensure that all stripes will be of equal size and that the same color stripe is on the top and bottom. Eight- to twelve-inch stripes are visually pleasing to the eye.

3. Use a measuring tape and a pencil to measure and mark the size of the stripes from the ceiling down to the baseboard. Then use a level (a laser level is ideal) to precisely mark lines in pencil across the width. Ceilings aren't always straight, so use the level as your guide.

4. Carefully apply painter's tape just above the top pencil line and just below the second pencil line and then continue down the wall for the rest of the stripes. Make sure you taped inside the base-colored stripes, exposing the full area of wall intended for alternate stripes.

5. Seal the tape so the stripe color won't bleed. For example, if you're using a semi-gloss white for your alternate stripe as I did, paint your base color paint right over the edges of your tape in the area where you're going to paint white stripes. As it dries it seals the tape so that your white paint won't bleed under into the gray and make the stripes all wonky!

6. Paint your stripes and remove the tape to reveal perfectly crisp lines!

WHAT YOU'LL NEED:
paint brush
paint
tape measure
level
pencil
painter's tape

Function and Style in Small Spaces

When you look around your home, you'll realize there are in-between spaces where much of life happens. The obstacle to giving these spaces a refresh is that they are spaces we *need* to use. It becomes easy to put off doing anything new to them for that one reason.

I have good news. Tending to these vital areas in our home doesn't require a lot of paint or lighting or window treatments (a lot of these spaces don't *have* windows!). Your makeover to-do list can be short. You can also add special touches over time so that you don't inconvenience yourself or your family.

A little love, effort, and style will go a long way. And the result will be appreciated daily in these functional spaces.

START HERE

If you want to organize your house, first consider how you are and are not making the best use of your space. In what way is your house not functioning well? What in-between spaces have gone ignored? Could you solve the problem with a little creative thinking or reorganizing the space?

Look at all small areas with fresh eyes to consider how you can add personal style and organizational helps to make them enjoyable and intentional.

To add personality and a nod to our love for travel, we pinned up heavy-duty gift wrap printed with maps of the places we've visited.

KEEPING IT REAL

Without my command center, I'd be THAT mom more often. In fact, the reason I had to get a board like this is because I WAS that mom. Yep, I was the one who took her son back to school after spring break—three days before the break ended. I was also the one who forgot to order school pictures two years in a row because I lost the order form.

A Small Hallway

Some small spaces are seen as too small to be useful. But our small hallway proves otherwise.

With two self-employed, busy parents running startup businesses in our home and organizing a family of five (including a middle schooler), we can accumulate a lot of paper and stuff. Surprised? I'm guessing not.

To manage life, it's essential for us to have systems for organizing schedules and papers and for displaying reminders. In our home, our much-used hallway became just the place to set up our area for communication and organization. It helps us get our act together—some days at least!

Everyday on Display— A Command Center

In the little hallway outside my kitchen, I have what we call our "command central." It's a simple magnetic blackboard we use for our most urgent papers. The board is located right in the main hub of our house so we don't lose or forget something important. Here we keep important papers and lists, pens, paperclips, and notepads, and we also display and store seasonal decor.

Forest Park—
Tillamook NW23rd
Mt Hood Powell's
Haystack
West Hills Rock
Hawthorne
Willamette ValleY

Laundry Room

Our laundry room was at the bottom of our to-do list for more than five years. Finally we made the time to give it a quick refresh. Although it's a small and simple space, it's the most luxurious laundry area I have had. We've had a small closet with a stacked washer and dryer and a few dark basement laundry rooms, so this one makes me very happy.

Consider which of your daily task spaces needs attention. Don't become overwhelmed with a long list of fixes. Keep to a simple plan. In our laundry room, we painted the walls a fresh coat of white, created a window shade (see Embellish!), replaced the unfortunate fluorescent light with a fun green barn light, added big baskets for organization, and brought in a happy striped runner we already had. I had dreams of subway tiles and a new sink, but my practical side won out, and I opted for simplicity! I'm so glad I did.

We use this room every single day, so it was high time it got a little love.

AFTER

BEFORE

Embellish!

{NO-SEW ROLL-UP SHADE}

Add style to a functional space with easy-to-make window shades. For a finishing detail, we created a roll-up shade that is rather stationary but can be adjusted by loosening the twine.

1 Hang a curtain rod that is a couple of inches wider than your window opening, using wall anchors for stability if necessary. We placed our rod near the ceiling to give the illusion of a bigger window and showing more fabric without blocking too much light.

2 Put the curtain panel on the rod and let the curtain hang down, covering the window.

3 Cut your rope or ribbon about two feet long. You can trim the excess later if necessary.

4 Roll the fabric evenly (backwards) so the pattern will remain visible. You may need some extra hands for this step and especially the next one, depending on how wide your fabric is.

5 While keeping your fabric rolled (using an extra set of hands or pins), tie the rope around the rod and in a knot or bow at the bottom of the rolled fabric.

6 Roll fabric tighter, higher, or lower and adjust the rope horizontally so the curtain hangs straight. If you won't be unrolling the shade, use push pins to help the fabric hang against the wall. If your fabric misbehaves, roll it around a lightweight dowel or cafe rod for added stiffness.

TIP: Premade panels are often in widths of 48 or 54 inches. We used one 54-inch panel. If your window is wide, use multiple panels or regular fabric and sew your own rod pocket or tabs.

5 Things Every Small Space Needs

1. Furniture That Maximizes Space

The right shape and style of furniture can make a small space as functional, attractive, and comfortable as a large space. Here are some of our favorites:

- Small Scale & Armless
- Tall & Narrow
- Round Shapes
- Nesting Tables
- Dropleaf & Casters
- Corner Pieces
- Dual Function (i.e. storage ottoman)

2. Wall Hooks and Shelves

When you have limited square footage or closet space, add wall hooks for bags, coats, and keys. Consider wall shelves to hold display items. Choose solutions your family will use so you can keep clutter off the floor and surfaces clear.

3. Layers and Texture

Make the most of the cozy potential of your small room by adding textures you love! If your space is a bedroom or family area, add several pillows, a warm textured throw, and floor-to-ceiling drapery so you'll feel tucked into your nest.

4. Light

If your small room is lacking in natural light, add layers of lighting! For example, you might have an overhead light, a plug-in sconce clipped to shelves or posts, and an accent lamp on a table. Use various sources to create a very pleasant ambience.

5. Reflection

Add a mirror to your small space. Any light that does stream in will reflect, and the depth of image from the reflection will make your space look bigger.

Even the smallest nooks and crannies of a home can be improved to offer more style and function.

7

A Sanctuary for the Seasons

{A Home Year Round}

Evolving our home throughout the seasons with simple refinements can enhance our everyday experiences all year round and inspire us to live more fully in each moment.

Each of us may gravitate toward a particular season's style for a variety of reasons. Perhaps we prefer the climate of one season, or we're inspired by our region during certain months, or we hold special childhood memories of a particular season.

Whatever our preferences, a well-loved home is enjoyed throughout the year. By allowing our spaces to reflect the mood and ambience each season represents, we can be oh-so-cozy in fall and winter with a warm and natural style, and then we can have our spirits lifted by the bright colors and freshness of spring and summer.

Making simple changes is the best way to fall in love—and stay in love—with your home throughout the year.

LET THE SEASONS
INSPIRE YOUR DECOR

DELIGHT THE SENSES
WITH A COFFEE
STATION

DIY—CAPTURE
A WINTER
WONDERLAND

The Cozy Home

In the fall and winter months, it's all about nesting to create a warm and inviting home. I think the simplest ways are the easiest. Bring out the soft layers that tempt you to nestle in. Stacks of fluffy pillows and throws in different textures, colors, and patterns will not only warm you up, but they add a comfy layer to the backs of sofas and chairs.

When temperatures start to drop, a blazing fireplace will make you feel extra snug and warm. If you don't have a fireplace, consider a freestanding electric model to bring a sense of warmth and ambience to your home.

Bring in natural elements. A simple or festive wreath on the front door is the perfect way to welcome guests (and yourself!) home. Boxwood is a great year-round option, but it's especially wonderful for winter greenery! The treasures that go with fall will nurture your home and family.

My list of favorite things about this season goes on and on.

START HERE

Which season is your favorite? How does it influence your home and your family rituals? Think about how touches of each season could brighten your rooms, make them more inviting, echo special memories, and inspire you to love your home all year round.

Everyday on Display— A Coffee Station

Yes, the aroma and taste of great coffee are wonderful, but creating a beautiful *destination* for that ritual makes the daily experience all the better. This is "everyday on display" at its best.

We are big coffee fans, which is nearly a requirement when living in the Pacific Northwest. So it's no surprise that one of my coziest home features in any season is our coffee station. It is enjoyable to choose a special mug, add in a seasonal flavor, and take a moment to appreciate the gifts that the cycle of the year brings. *See how to personalize your station later in this chapter.*

—FALL—

- Enjoy the light of candles flickering at dinnertime.

- Breathe in the great scents of cinnamon, oranges, and cloves.

- Use pumpkins and other colorful gourds for decor.

- Tuck pinecones and sprigs of evergreen throughout the house.

- Cook up a batch of chili and corn bread smothered in honey.

- Delight in the wind blowing through leaves—bring some of the leaves and branches inside.

- Play board games while eating popcorn or caramel apples.

- Settle in to fluffy feather beds on a cold night.

- Introduce autumn hues of amber, yellow, and copper.

Okay, that list just made me a little hungry and sleepy. How about you? Ah, the pleasures of fall.

A Personalized Coffee Station

No matter the season, create a space that welcomes you, your family, and your guests to indulge in a freshly brewed cup of coffee. With a few steps, you can set up your own coffee station on a counter, a roller cart, or anywhere you have room.

Container of your favorite coffee

Choose a pretty jar or canister and fill it with really good coffee. Some of my favorites include Stumptown Coffee, Sleepy Monk, and Storyville Coffee Roasters. Have a coffee scoop in or near the jar. Don't forget other beverage favorites that suit the season. Fill a container with hot chocolate and tea packets!

Coffeemaker

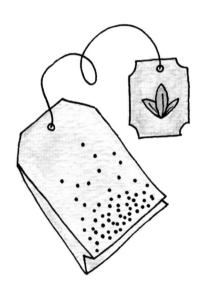

By "coffeemaker" I don't mean a live-in barista! But wouldn't that be nice? The appliance you have doesn't have to be fancy—anything from a drip coffeemaker to a French Press to a Nespresso will do.

Mugs and a mug tree

Mix and match different mugs for an eclectic look or go classic with simple white mugs. What's more fun than finding a special mug (or receiving one) and then displaying it?

Personalized taste mini station: cream, sugar, and syrup

Provide options for every personal taste with cream, sugar, and flavored syrups. Don't forget seasonal coffee and syrup flavors. Place syrup bottles on the counter (or make your syrup and use glass oil dispensers for a clean look), in a wine bottle rack, or in a basket that can be moved if you need the counter space.

A pretty towel or napkins

Hang towels and stack pretty napkins near your coffee station to bring a touch of seasonal color to your kitchen. We made our own rod to hang towels by sliding a long branch through shelf brackets.

A cookie jar

Baked goodies make an afternoon sip of java even more delightful. Keep a jar nearby of biscotti, cookies, sweet biscuits, or other family favorites for a tasty coffee break.

Accessorize for Your Senses

Have you ever thought of aromas as a seasonal accessory? Why not? The cooler months are especially fun to "decorate" with yummy scents. You can enhance the cozy factor with freshly baked cookies, lit candles in seasonal fragrances, and one of my favorites, spiced cider simmering on the stove.

Hot Spiced Cranberry Cider

8 cups cranberry juice (not cocktail, just cranberry juice)

8 cups good quality apple cider (get it fresh from the farm if you can)

2-4 tablespoons brown sugar

4 cinnamon sticks

Pinch of allspice

8 whole cloves

Orange slices with peel (wash oranges and then slice)

In a large pot, mix all of the ingredients together. Heat until the liquid begins to simmer and then reduce heat and continue simmering until the brown sugar has melted. Taste the cider and adjust as needed (it may need a bit more brown sugar). Strain out the cloves before serving.

TIP: Special scents do wonders for your home's ambience even as the sun begins to shine. Which aromas trigger happy memories of childhood or travel? Maybe it is lilac in spring? Or coconut in summer? Bring those scents inside your home now as you make new memories.

Christmas Cheer

Around the holidays, our home evolves even more. Traditions are something to look forward to! Whether we go all out with festivity or keep things subtle and natural, our home can inspire us to celebrate and remember what each season represents.

Living in the Pacific Northwest, my home is literally nestled between the forest and the sea. These landscapes inspire me during the Christmas season. Fresh greenery, natural elements, and subtle references to our region are blended with a few touches of sparkle, making my home feel magical but still natural and comfortable. I tend to keep things simple at Christmas as I bring in warm touches in layers:

- layers of winter linens on the table

- baskets filled with throw blankets (try plaid and extra thick knits!)

- seasonal art or tapestries on walls for layers of warmth

- nooks for reading holiday stories

- warm area rugs in living spaces and by the bed

Incorporating elements you love will add the right amount of cheer for the season without too much fuss. You want your sanctuary to be stress-free so you can savor this special time of year.

—WINTER—

- Drape wreaths, ornaments, and lights on doors, beds, and mirrors.

- Hang Christmas stockings on mantels, stairways, or hooks around the house.

- Arrange shiny ornaments in bowls and trays.

- Add pinecones and mini trees to your decor.

- Inspire your family with Christmas verses written on a chalkboard.

- Lean a vintage sled in the entry or on the porch.

- Adorn windows with paper snowflakes.

- Display Christmas cards (new and vintage) throughout the house.

- Create homemade snow globes and place on shelves and windowsills.

KEEPING IT REAL

We crack up over animals with personalities all year round, so of course, we fill our tree with creatures and find its quirkiness to be perfectly suited to our sense of humor!

DIY: Charming Snow Globes

These snow globes are waterless and easy, and they add such a seasonal feel to your home over the holidays. I found an antique blue mason jar at a secondhand store that was perfect for a unique snow globe, but I love clear ones too.

What you need:
+ mason jars with lids
+ artificial snow from craft or garden stores
+ miniature figures of trees or other holiday items

1   Simply add a little bit of artificial snow to the bottom of the jar and set a small tree inside!

2   For the clear mason jar snow globe, we glued the tree to the lid before screwing it back together again and setting it upside down!

3   For a snowy look, add more snow to the jar while it is upright, and then screw on the lid and flip it over.

4   Get fancy and add cute little animals or add multiple small trees.

Bring in Spring

Spring is a beautiful time to lighten up and refresh your spaces.

Year round, I love decorating with a collection of blue glass bottles and mason jars. In spring I combine them with a bouquet of flowers, and in the summer, they make me think about the beach, so I often add sand and shells. The colored glass is a perfect transitional collection between the seasons!

Consider what accessories and furnishings you have that can help you bridge the seasons with cheer. With a few simple touches, your home can reflect the emerging colors and the freshness that spring inspires!

-SPRING-

- Change bedding to fresh white or summery sheets and lightweight blankets.

- Place lively plants and flowers on the mantel or anchor cabinet for a cheery focal point.

- Put bowls of colorful fruit in the kitchen.

- Set the table with springy dishes and patterned cloth napkins.

- Use bouquets of tulips in pitchers for the dining tables.

- Fill glass hurricanes or bowls with decorative eggs in soft colors for a fresh centerpiece!

- Plant flowers in a hanging basket, a wood crate, or in old metal buckets.

- Browse through garden stores for inspiration. I love walking along crushed-gravel pathways looking at pretty plants. It's therapeutic.

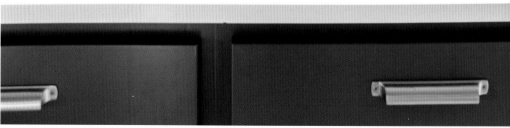

A Summer House

I am happy when skies are blue, the air is warm, and colorful flowers are blooming! Summer lifts my spirits and inspires me to evoke that same mood in my home.

One of the first things I do is remove things from the cooler seasons. I enjoy this experience as much as I enjoyed adding in those cozier items months before. Putting away the heavier layers of winter is refreshing! Then I usher in the new season with glimpses of color and brighter accessories to lift the mood of the house and its inhabitants! One of the benefits to my home's generally neutral color scheme in paint and furnishings is being able to mix things up by adding a new color for the seasons.

Consider what makes your home a summer house. Do you have a porch or balcony that becomes a favorite space to enjoy lemonade or moments in the sun? What do you clear out and what do you add in to reflect the joy of this season?

—SUMMER—

- Refresh shelves to reflect new seasonal hues. I bring in summer accessories, such as my favorite whale platter or other nautical decor.

- Brighten your everyday on display options. I rearrange my cookbooks according to seasonal favorites to inspire me.

- Brighten the bedroom with floral pillow shams.

- Add vibrant paper lanterns to your yard or a family space for summer style.

- Embrace the small thrill of bringing home a cute new hand towel or pitcher.

- Set out bright bowls for serving and entertaining.

- Gather up pretty books and stack them for summer reading.

- Roll up the winter rugs. Expose bare wood floors or change to lighter cotton rugs in summery stripes and colors.

- Place flowers in vases and pitchers or float blossoms in glass bowls.

Love Where You Live

{Closing}

There is endless advice in magazines, books, and blogs for what makes a lovely home—and how to go about creating one. Though when it comes down to what matters, our vision of a sanctuary and how we create it is very personal.

It's freeing to be able to find your own style and express who you are, even if experts, neighbors, or salespeople try to convince you to change. Remember that others may be in a different place in life, have different goals or insights, or appreciate beauty in things you've never considered. But rather than feeling like your home doesn't measure up, it is far more enjoyable to do our own thing and do it well.

My advice? Be authentic. We have to follow our own path to a home we love. Embrace your own unique style. Be so "out" you are "in." Be willing to take risks and embrace those happy accidents. Celebrate each time you try something new. Give yourself grace for the season you are in. Little by little your home will be the haven you envision.

Love where you live, and your home will inspire your life.

that house was...'a perfect house,
whether you like food or sleep,
or story-telling or singing, or just
sitting and thinking best,
or a pleasant mixture of them all'.
Merely to be there
was a cure for weariness,
fear, and sadness.

J.R.R. TOLKIEN

DETAILS, DETAILS

184

Studio Taupe

BEHR ALL-IN-ONE

White Dove

BENJAMIN MOORE

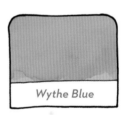

Wythe Blue

BENJAMIN MOORE
(door exterior)

Kendall Charcoal

BENJAMIN MOORE
(door interior)

ENTRY

Furniture & Accessories

1. White and gray rug—Dash & Albert

2. Black light above coat hooks—Lowe's Home Improvement

3. Coat hooks—Rejuvenation

4. Mirrors—Target

Not Pictured: blue ceramic lamp (HomeGoods), chandelier before embellishment (Hampton Bay), stairway sconces (Elk Lighting), green painted table (secondhand)

GATHERING ROOM

Studio Taupe

BEHR ALL-IN-ONE

Furniture & Accessories

1 Linen settee—Elliot Settee by Birch Lane

2 Wood stools with painted legs—Serena and Lily

3 White curtains—IKEA

4 Light taupe glass cabinet—Restoration Hardware

5 Wood lamps—Target

6 Pharmacy lamp—J.C. Penney

7 Settee pillows—World Market

Flea Market & Secondhand Finds: globe, wooden armchair, dresser, ottoman, blue water jug, elephant

DINING ROOM

Furniture & Accessories

1 Table—Pottery Barn

2 Wood and metal console—World Market

3 Zigzag wood cabinet—Pier 1 Imports

4 Mirror above patterned wood cabinet—HomeGoods

5 Copper Lantern—Pottery Barn

6 Metal and wicker chairs—World Market

7 Gray wingback chairs—World Market

8 White plates (select ones)—HomeGoods

Flea Market & Secondhand Finds: brass horses, select white plates, Turkish towel, round side table, curtains

White Dove

BENJAMIN MOORE

KITCHEN

Furniture & Accessories

1 Freestanding dish cabinet—Homegoods

2 Blinds—Bamboo Tortoise, Select Blinds

3 Island stain—Jacobean, Minwax

4 Mugs—Anthropologie

Not Pictured: round wood mirror (Lulu & Georgia), brass and mirror knobs (Anthropologie), rattan chairs (secondhand), copper pots (secondhand)

Surfaces

5 Cabinets—Huntwood

6 Wood flooring—Natural Hickory, Mohawk

7 Quartz countertops—Organic White, Caesarstone

8 Subway tile—Arctic White, Daltile

9 Tile grout—Oyster Gray, Polyblend

10 Sink—Whitehaven short apron front, Kohler

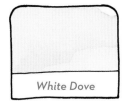

White Dove

BENJAMIN MOORE
(upper cabinets, plank walls,
island base, and trim)

Polished Limestone

GLIDDEN
(ceiling)

Polished Grey

GLIDDEN (lightened version
of Glidden Wood Smoke)
(kitchen and pantry)

Kendall Charcoal

BENJAMIN MOORE
(lower cabinets)

Hardware & Lighting

Satin nickel pulls—Duluth Pulls, Restoration Hardware

Island brass fox and bunny knobs—Anthropologie

Faucet—Danze

Range hood—Zephyr Anzio, 30-inch

Espresso machine—Jura Capresso Impressa S9

Metal wall sconces—Restoration Hardware

Ceiling lights (not shown)—Barn Light Electric

FAMILY ROOM

Polished Grey

GLIDDEN (lightened version of Glidden Wood Smoke)

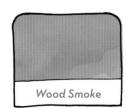

Wood Smoke

GLIDDEN

Furniture & Accessories

1 Gray wingback—Ballard Designs

2 Trellis brown wingback—Pier 1 Imports

3 Mirror above fireplace—Restoration Hardware

4 Cabinet—Restoration Hardware

5 Glass lamps—HomeGoods

6 Tufted Ottoman—World Market

7 Wood tray on ottoman—LoveFeast

8 Striped rug—Lulu & Georgia

Flea Market & Secondhand Finds: green garden stool, antique paddles

Not Pictured: gold accent tables flanking fireplace (Pier 1 Imports), glass and gold lamps (Target), leather sofa (Pottery Barn)

MASTER BEDROOM

Furniture & Accessories

1 Bed—Ethan Allen (secondhand)

2 Mirror—HomeGoods

3 Blue-gray nightstand—Joss & Main

4 Bedside lamps—Safavieh from Overstock

5 Curtains—World Market

6 White duvet—Target

7 Navy pillow shams—Anthropologie

8 Embroidered navy and white pillow shams—Williams Sonoma Home

Flea Market & Secondhand Finds: grain sack pillow

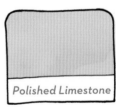

Polished Limestone

GLIDDEN

Not Pictured: settee (Birch Lane), armoire (Ethan Allen), chinoiserie black cabinet (family heirloom), canvas art above black cabinet (World Market), verse art (Between You and Me, Etsy), gold nightstand (Joss & Main)

OFFICE

Hale Navy

BENJAMIN MOORE

Flea Market & Secondhand Finds: white secretary and hutch, rattan bookshelf

Not Pictured: brass sconces (Lite Source)

Furniture & Accessories

1 Desk—Pottery Barn

2 White drawers—IKEA

3 Lamps—Safavieh from Overstock

4 Curtains—Anthropologie

5 Yellow chair—World Market

6 Desk chair—Restoration Hardware

To find more details on products and furnishings in our home and many of our favorite decorating sources, please visit theinspiredroom.net/shop.

Dreams & Details

_____

_____

_____

_____

_____

_____

_____

_____

_____

_____

_____

_____

_____

_____

_____

_____

Let's Connect

Melissa Michaels, *New York Times* bestselling author of *Love the Home You Have* and *The Inspired Room*, is the creator of the popular, award-winning blog The Inspired Room. She lives with her husband, son, and two cute pups in the Pacific Northwest. They live near their two daughters, who are also an active part of The Inspired Room.

Connect with Melissa and other home-lovers daily through The Inspired Room (theinspiredroom.net). Sign up on the blog for free content and inspiration delivered right to your inbox.

You are invited to share your own adventures of creating a home and be inspired by the stories of others at Melissa's new community blog site, Home Love Stories (homelovestories.com).

Follow Melissa on social media at Facebook.com/theinspiredroom.fans, and as theinspiredroom on Instagram, Pinterest, and Twitter.

HOME LOVE STORIES

It's Free!

Join Our Community

As a blogger at The Inspired Room and an author, I share my home and life with anyone who wants to read about them. But the truth is, I really just want you all to move in next door to me so I can get to know YOUR stories.

Home Love Stories is a community to get together and share about our homes and our lives. It's free. And you don't have to have a blog or be a pro at social media. (If you do have a blog, think of this as your vacation home.) It's just easy and fun! This is a no-fuss, keeping-it-real place where we can laugh about our mistakes and celebrate our big and small moments. Come on over.

- Be part of a community of home-lovers
- Share what you love about your home
- Join in on weekly home challenges and block parties
- Gather inspiration from others
- Interact with me and new friends from all over

Let's Be Neighbors!

Follow @HomeLoveStories on Instagram to keep up with fun announcements!

Join us today at HomeLoveStories.com

Home Is Right Where You Are

Join Melissa Michaels of The Inspired Room to transform your rooms (and your life) as you discover the beauty in the ordinary and how to go from dreamer to doer with ease. Each step of the way, Melissa offers encouragement and personal stories to help you

- discover your style and let it shine with simple ideas
- create and organize rooms with purpose and intention
- gather inspiration in the 31-day Love Your Home Challenge

Fall in love with the home you have and embrace the gifts of life, people, and blessings right where you are.

NEW YORK TIMES Bestseller

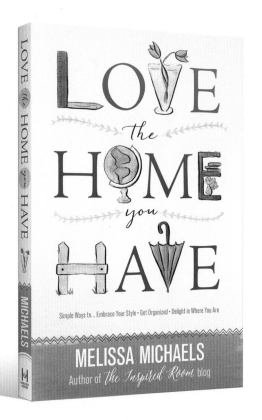

Melissa Michaels, how did you get into my every house-obsessed thought?

—**Jill Waage,** Executive Editor, Better Homes and Gardens Brand

Melissa's thoughtful call to contentment comes complete with helpful tips and action items, but more than anything, it gives us permission to embrace imperfections.

—**Sophie Hudson,** author of *Home Is Where My People Are* and blogger at BooMama.net

Love the Home You Have is charming, witty, and gracious. Melissa gives all of us Pinterest lovers (yes, that's me!) the freedom to let our homes evolve day-to-day, season-to-season.

—**Sandy Coughlin,** author and founder of ReluctantEntertainer.com

Style Notes

Want to fly through your cleaning routine? Sorry to disappoint you (and me), but PJs tell us to be lazy and maybe even crawl back in bed. Aprons tell me it is okay to tackle a quick cleaning job regardless of what I'm wearing. Super-nice clothes tell me I shouldn't clean at all. What we wear can affect our efficiency! Getting dressed tells us to get busy. Moral of this—get dressed, and I bet you'll be more efficient. Try it!

Most of us are encouraged and inspired by a pleasantly clean and tidy house whether we work in or out of the home. We don't want to obsess over cleanliness, but we do need to make basic routines a priority in our day.

Let's make housekeeping as simple as possible. We can't spend all day cleaning or trying to keep up with lofty expectations. I have a life to live and so do you. I truly believe that if we simplify our expectations we will thrive and be able to accomplish what we want.

Remember your priorities so you can be realistic about what "clean enough" means for you. If your priorities are to raise and nurture your young family, you know that beautiful messes will happen daily in this season of your life. Embrace them! If you are building a career, recognize that you won't have much time to invest in your home. If you are serving others and impacting the world, your daily routines will give you the energy and motivation to keep on being your awesome self! A clean-enough house empowers us to *be more*—while doing less to stay ahead of the chaos.

Be Consistent

The key to successful housekeeping is to turn daily routines into doable habits so you have time to enjoy the fruit of your labor. When you experience a clean-enough house for a couple months in a row, you'll be inspired to keep up the momentum and envision new possibilities for your home and life!

You'll feel better and more in control after each little housekeeping win! Every time you make the bed, you'll be pleased to see it as you pass by. Every day you polish up your sink, you'll be happier. Those are little victories. And consistent little victories add up to the bigger win, which starts to unfold after you've been doing your routines for a month.

Consistency with daily cleaning frenzies is one of the secrets to a clean-enough house. We can do them anytime we have a few moments.

A clean-enough HOUSE EMPOWERS US TO be more while doing less to STAY AHEAD OF THE CHAOS

31-DAY
Love Your Home
CHALLENGE

DAY 1
{ HOME GRATITUDE }

Your home is a gift and a blessing. Walk around your house and think about how thankful you are for a roof over your head. In spite of all its quirks and imperfections, your home is where you can create a place to nurture yourself and bless your family. Try not to worry about all the material things you want to buy or change or improve. Instead, remember how blessed you are to be able to create a home full of memories with what you already have. View each room through the lens of gratitude for the life you can create and memories you can make in your home!

What room or memory stands out as a blessing today?

_____

DAY 2
{ DECLUTTER }

What's the very first spot that comes to mind when you think of the most cluttered drawer or closet in your home? The kitchen drawer full of junk you never use? The closet with an avalanche of clothes? Clutter takes up space, making daily routines more challenging. Give yourself the gift of a less cluttered life. Choose one small area you can tackle today. Turn on some music and create order in one spot in your home!

Which area did you declutter? How did you feel while taking this step toward organization?

_____
_____

Acknowledgments

Big heartfelt thanks to the many people who inspired this book and helped bring it to life!

Thank you...

To my talented and enthusiastic team at Harvest House Publishers. Thanks to each and every one of you for your kindness and for always going above and beyond to create something special. Extra thanks to Heather for her coordination of this project and to Nicole for creating beautiful artwork. It is a joy to work with you.

To Hope, my friend and hardworking editor, thank you for making sense of what I want to say. P.S. I think you are right. After we are done training with books, we just might have a bright future at the circus on the flying trapeze! I'll meet you by the elephants.

To my behind-the-scenes cheerleader and agent, Ruth, thank you for the support and the confidence you have in my work.

To the designers at Faceout Studio, the opportunity to collaborate with you has been amazing!

To my favorite groups of ladies: the Divas, (in)courage, and the wonderful friends who have generously shown me overwhelming support and kindness along the way.

Thank you to my husband, Jerry, not only for the valiant effort in dust bunny chasing during the photography for this book but for your enthusiasm and love every step of the way. This is livin'!

To Courtney, my middle daughter and partner in crime and creativity, I'm grateful beyond words for your help. Thank you for the laughs, encouragement, and motivational pep talks.

To Kylee, my oldest daughter and valued part of our trio, thank you for your persistent attempts to bring order and artistry to the chaos. We are always better when we are together, so I'm grateful to Lance for sharing you with us.

To Luke, my most handsome and best son, thank you for fixing everything the rest of us break with your sharp mind, strong arms, and creative talent. You are a special snowflake.

Thank you to my sister, Heather, for offering your help along the way and of course, the periodic fits of laughter over random things like necks.

And last but definitely not least, thanks, Mom and Dad, for basically everything!